YOUR CHILD
MEETS THE WORLD OUTSIDE

Helping children develop the basic attitudes of democratic living may do more than anything else to bring us nearer the ideal of democracy.

YOUR CHILD MEETS THE WORLD OUTSIDE

*A Guide to Children's Attitudes
in Democratic Living*

By

ELIZABETH F. BOETTIGER

With an Introduction by
JESSIE STANTON

D. APPLETON-CENTURY COMPANY
INCORPORATED

New York   London

1941

COPYRIGHT, 1941, BY

D. APPLETON-CENTURY COMPANY, INC.

PRINTED IN THE UNITED STATES OF AMERICA

-14

TO THE MEMORY OF
My FATHER

Foreword

LONG A TEACHER OF SMALL CHILDREN, A KEEN OBSERVER of the way they grow and develop, Miss Boettiger began to write when illness put an end to her teaching. A student not only of children but also of the civilization in which they live, she wrote from a deep interest in the interaction between the child and this complex modern environment.

We know that not only in classrooms but in after-school play and, most of all, in their life at home, children are constantly exploring relationships, trying to find out how the world wags, and are continually working out ways to deal with it to their own satisfaction. We know that long before he reaches school age, in fact, from the moment he comes into the world, a child begins this exploration and is already establishing his character—his own way of living in the world he discovers. More and more we realize that these earliest learnings are never forgotten, are not put away like childish things, but remain deep in each person's character and greatly affect his later learnings.

To many parents these notions are challenging but vague. It is hard enough to think definitely just what a youngster *is* learning, out of everyday family life, that will affect him deeply. It is still harder to think definitely what experiences he should be getting, and how we can see to it that he does get them.

This book offers stimulus and help to parents in formulating their own ideas of the kind of world we live in. This means (since life is neither static nor simple) seeing some trends that we would like to strengthen, some we hope to curb. It is the first step toward knowing what kind of experiences will give our children a good start. Then the question is: What can we do to make family living rich in these experiences? Miss Boettiger offers many illustrations in which parents will recognize the stuff that everyday home life is made of. But here we begin to see unsuspected importance in the seemingly trivial choices we are constantly making in haste and almost without purpose.

In her chapter on "Our Attitudes toward Other People: The Roots of Intolerance," Miss Boettiger says that "the first principle of democracy is that individuals are valuable for themselves and for what they contribute to the commonweal." Then, because she acted on this principle in teaching children, she takes it for granted that we carry this over into family life. But this point should be re-emphasized, for we are coming more and more to understand that it is essential to accept a child as he is, at each stage of his development, giving him a sense of belonging to his family just because he is himself, which gives him that sense of security, of inner peace and strength, which will enable him as he grows older to accept people who are different from himself. Tolerance for others grows, in part, from acceptance of one's self.

Miss Boettiger has written a timely book, a book full of practical help toward a sounder basis for making choices and planning new experiences in the family and in the community which will fit our children to undertake more fully and successfully the responsibilities of citizenship in a democracy.

JESSIE STANTON

Acknowledgment

ACKNOWLEDGMENT IS GRATEFULLY GIVEN TO MISS MARY
Phelps, Secretary of the Writers Laboratory, Bank Street
Schools, for her very helpful criticism and editorial suggestions in the preparation of this book. The following
schools have been of real assistance in the matter of illustrations: the Manumit School, Pawling, New York; the
Hessian Hills School, Croton-on-Hudson, New York; the
City and Country School, the Little Red School House, and
the Bank Street Schools, New York City.

Contents

IV. The Outside World of People

V. The Outside Community World

Illustrations

I

Families and the World Outside: an Introduction

I

Families and the World Outside

ONCE A SMALL BOY AND HIS FATHER WERE WALKING through city streets. They passed a Protestant church, then a Catholic church, then a Jewish synagogue. The father explained in simple terms how there were people who met together in each of these places because of the things they believed about the world, about themselves, and about other people. Suddenly the small boy took hold of his father's hand and asked earnestly: "Daddy, what do you believe? I want to believe what you believe."

Most parents, at one time or another, are thus confronted with their job, and most of us, so challenged, can not help feeling a little hollow inside. For we realize, in a flash, what important people parents really are. We realize that the emotional ties that exist in families give our attitudes and explanations a distinct prestige, a prestige that is enjoyed by no other social group except under pressure.

People act and think within the limits of accepted social and religious standards, not with complete freedom. The family has always played its part in the transmission of these accepted standards. In a society such as ours, where customs change so rapidly, where different ways of doing and acting are so mixed, one would expect families to feel themselves increasingly important in this respect. But this is not always the case. The year-old child may be taught to fold his hands while his mother recites the Lord's Prayer; yet this same youngster, and his older brothers and sisters, may be exposed to the many products of our heterogeneous world—the mechanical toys, the radio, the printed matter, the movies—without any thought-out basis for discrimination and approach. Even about those customs which have the prestige of long usage we are not always consistent. Grown-up members of a family may seldom go to church, yet children may be sent regularly to a church school.

A baby's existence goes on entirely within the bounds of his family. Everything that approaches him has been thoroughly censored, has only filtered through from the outside. As soon as he gets on his own two feet, however, his boundaries begin to grow. The outside world in many forms comes pressing in upon him. To-day, more than ever, families are important in the give and take that then ensues. Let us explore why.

In all the recent talk about democracy and its aims, there is a special significance for parents. All people who conscientiously try to define the difference between a democratic and a totalitarian way of living are agreed that fundamentally it is a question of responsibility. In a totalitarian state, individuals are told what to do and how to think; in a democracy, they are expected, within the social framework, to think and act for themselves.

But no one can think and act independently out of thin

air. Independence is a state into which one grows. The little boy who wanted to believe what his father believed was going through a natural and very necessary stage of this growth. If family living is a success, the ways of behaving, the habits of thought which are a part of it, will become part of a child's personality as he matures. They form for him a kind of inner regulator, affecting what is done or not done throughout a lifetime, without conscious or reasoned thought. Independent thinking will extend and modify these first attitudes, but by and large they are there to stay.

A democracy relies on people's inner attitudes much more than on the external regulators, laws and forces. Individuals are left as free as possible. Laws are not for regimenting but for assuring to every one the chance to realize his capacities. In modern life, each person's behavior affects many others. The lasting attitudes that begin in family living are therefore of crucial importance. Families are really the center, the core, around which our democratic society is built. In a world which challenges democratic living, then, parents have an added responsibility. The job of setting standards, of developing attitudes, is no mean one—and it can not begin too early. Even the toddler begins to feel the impact of, begins to assimilate, the outside world.

If children are to be helped to develop attitudes consistently, there must be within the family a clearly defined way of doing and thinking which is recognized as *our* way. A little child relies heavily upon this simple acceptance of standards, and it must be firmly there for him to lean upon. It is an important part of his bulwark of security. "*Our* house has a sun porch." "*We* take turns helping Tina with her dishes." Recognized behavior, as well as possessions, can help to bolster young egos.

As children grow older, family ways that are definite are helpful in another way. There comes a time when children desire above all else to be part of the crowd, to conform. It is very important what other people do, how they dress, how they behave. Conformity is a necessary part of early adolescence. But in his desire to be "one of the crowd," the young adolescent may be all too willing to forfeit his own independence. The opposition that conscientious parents often have to give can, if wisely exerted, help children resist this undue group pressure. By maintaining family standards (and here a carefully thought-out point of view helps to give one the courage of convictions), we can help young people keep a salutary balance for which, in the long run, they may be extremely grateful.

Out of family living itself comes the solidarity that gives meaning to *our* way. It is a happy combination of affectionate companionship and recognized authority. Other ways of doing things will often appear attractive, to be sure. "But, Mother, *why* can't I? Jimmy does!" Most parents have heard this plea many times. There are many things that Jimmy does. He goes to the movies every Saturday; he spends his allowance on cheap candy; he climbs the fence into the ball-field when the policeman isn't looking. Almost every boy or girl has some neighborhood playmate, usually a bit older, whom he wants to copy, wants to be like. The Jimmys are often a problem.

However, if our reasons for not wanting children to do certain things are sound, if they are carefully thought out, then we will continue not to want those things done, no matter what other children do. Every family has to be prepared for some strain of this kind. Perhaps the best preparation is the attitude we ourselves take. The fact that *we* do such and such, that *we* only go to the movies as a family treat, or do not get paid for cutting the lawn, is not a deprivation. It is *our* way.

There will be grievances, unavoidably. One little girl, after such a difference of opinion, asked her mother: "Mommy, when I grow up and have children, will you say what they can do?" On being assured that her mother would have nothing whatever to say on that subject, she went on: "Then I can tell you right now, they will wear socks!"

But resentments do not last when children and parents get on well together. For then solidarity has its positive as well as its negative side. The family that is used to working and playing together will be able to find ready substitutes for some of the forbidden joys. A workshop in the basement may prove much more interesting than weekly movies or aimless gatherings on street corners; looking forward to regular family trips may be ample recompense. If Jimmy can be invited to use the workshop or come on the trips, too, it may be possible to start a group of youngsters in a more desirable direction. For one must take the value of companionship into account, too.

Sometimes it is possible to have an understanding as

to desirable occupations among the parents of a neighborhood. I know of one street in a suburban community where four or five mothers met together for this purpose. Over the tea-cups they had the chance to tell each other the things they wished were different about "the gang's" activities. One mother objected to the large allowance that seemed necessary to meet demands; another was troubled by the neighborhood custom of keeping late bedtime hours; another by the attitude of intolerance which had sprung up against a new arrival.

By talking together, these mothers were able to work out a common ground of agreement in handling all these problems. Thus "the gang" soon met with a united front. Good styles as well as poor ones can be readily set, once there is an agreement as to procedure. Parent-teacher groups or similar organizations are sometimes the means of bringing these about. Open discussion helps us all to clarify our own ideas and to get the good of other opinions. But if concerted opinion is not possible, we may have to stick to our guns.

Although family standards have to be definite, they can not be exclusive. *Our* way is only the right way because it *is* ours, for a short time. It must stand the test of a wider outlook, too. Accepting standards on faith is a position that is being constantly outgrown. The whys and wherefores of other standards, other ways of doing and thinking, become, as soon as children are aware of them, equally important with their own. It is in attempts to understand these differences that the first uncritical acceptance of *our* way takes on meaning and depth. For it is only by evaluating, by comparing and judging, that any reasoned basis for behavior can be formed.

The standards established in family life are a valuable beginning, but they are only a beginning. Indeed, the family itself is only a beginning. As children mature, their allegiances and responsibilities inevitably branch out. First attitudes, therefore, must hold the possibilities of growth; they must lead out.

So it works both ways. First attitudes are important to democratic living; but democracy is also important to first attitudes. For in order that children may continue to grow, the environment roundabout them must be growing, too. It must be one upon which their new enthusiasms, their sturdy ideals, can operate. We do not, as some people seem to think, merely fit children to an existing world. We give them the tools with which to understand it, to be sure; but we also give them, whether we know it or not, an ability that is more than understanding—an ability to change it, to shape it toward their own ends. We have heard a lot recently about the dynamic nature of the totalitarian states. Democracies, too, are dynamic—and for this very reason: they give scope to growing minds.

It is just because the attitudes which we help children build up interact so closely with environment that we can not very well define desirable attitudes without exploring ultimate objectives. This is why, in the following pages, the long view prefaces details. But ultimate objectives are not easily defined. Each of us must, in the last analysis, work out his own. It is hoped that the ones outlined here, however, will be at least suggestive. They will have served a worth-while purpose if they do no more than emphasize how enormously the little day-by-day things we do can count.

II

The Outside World of Nature

I

Possible Attitudes toward the Natural World

THE WORLD OF NATURE IS ALL ABOUT US FROM BIRTH, the constant, though too often unconsidered, framework of our lives. No individuality, no weaving of personality into the social whole, can be complete without some recognition of it. Our attitude toward what is not human in our surroundings has, when all is said and done, a profound effect upon those thoughts and actions which are strictly social in character. Since this is so, we should ask what attitude toward the natural environment makes the soundest contribution for our purposes. What attitude toward nature helps to shape a democratic world?

Two quite different attitudes can be seen among us today. One is that of the manipulator, regarding nature primarily as raw material to be turned to men's uses. The other is that of the participator. In this view the natural world is a functioning thing; its processes must be appreciated and nurtured, not merely manipulated.

Does history show the social consequences of these attitudes?

Men have been manipulators since the time, ages ago, when they learned to herd animals and to cultivate plants.

But in those early times nature was not thought of as a raw material. It was felt to be, along with man himself, intimately bound up with the life of divine beings. Natural processes were used with wonder. The gods were adored that earth and man might be fertile.

Doubtless the more ruthless attitude of to-day had its beginnings when a new technic, mining, came into use. In the age of coal and iron—the age when men found sources of power in nature that made windmills and water-wheels seem feeble—mining gained a firm foothold in human economy. Agriculture had nourished in men the sense of renewal and a feeling of partnership in the miracle of nature's continual rebirth. Such feelings were no part of mining. Mining was use without nurture; it was exploitation.

Moreover, as mining gained sway, another new force, science, was remaking man's view of nature. In one area after another, universal law crowded out the gods whom men had petitioned. By the nineteenth century even living things, including man himself, fitted into a natural law—the law of evolution. Nature, men found, was "red in tooth and claw." Life was a struggle to survive, and victory crowned the most ruthless.

Both these sources—the practice of mining and the theory of evolution (in its first shocking form)—fed the exploiting attitude that still infects our life to-day. The social consequences are all too clear. Not only coal and iron but human beings have been exploited and depleted. The resulting social ills are too much a part of our daily lives to need elaboration here.

Man is of a piece with nature, according to scientific theory. Yet the habit of exploitation, partly fed by science, has isolated men from nature emotionally. The city dweller of to-day is a stranger in the natural world. Worse than that, he often has a sense of superiority to it. Even when recreation-bound, his excursions are often invasions. He builds his glaring roads to the tops of mountains. He strews his picnic refuse about. Not only the countryside but his own living suffers from such blindness. Human beings have to function from a wider base than just society can give them. If they are only exploiters, men can not reach those deep reservoirs of unhumanity which, as truly as the reservoirs that supply their cities with purifying water, could help to keep them sweet and clean.

The findings of science, if well digested, can reopen those reservoirs to us. The feeling of participation is truer to fact than the attitude of ruthless manipulation.

Primitive man felt himself a part of the natural environment because he invested it with his own vitality: he imagined it in terms of his own desires and limitations. Increasing knowledge has put us in much the same position, only now the tables are turned. We can think of ourselves as participants because we know that basically we are similar to everything else, rather than because we regard everything else as similar to us. We know that as we are distinct in our way, so other creatures are distinct in theirs, and that all of us are subject to the same universal laws. We are not strangers, nor merely lords of creation. We are creatures who have evolved the added responsibility of consciousness, a responsibility which gives into our hands the tasks of *understanding, ordering,* and *cherishing,* as well as utilizing, the larger whole of which we are a part. Man is rightly a user, but his using must be carried on from this point of view.

The sense of belonging, of being the responsible part of a natural environment, has profound effects upon social functioning. Just as the exploitation of natural resources has its counterpart in the exploitation of human beings, so conservation, the nurture and appreciation of nature, makes men more sensitive, more aware in their social lives.

Nature's emphasis is upon change, upon continuous becoming. But there is an underlying unity, a frame of reference, in which its birth and growth and birth again take place. To those for whom these natural rhythms are a conscious and ever-present part of living, the social scene is likewise dynamic. It is permeated with the same pregnant sense of becoming. Its frame of reference rests upon the same biological base.

Man is a species distinct in itself, with peculiar aptitudes and abilities to be developed. What this frame of natural reference means is that the vital issues of society are indeed vital, based as they are upon nurture, healthy living, and healthy growth. It means that we must understand our biological heritage well enough to set up the proper conditions for our own living. This includes care of the natural forces we have so carelessly disturbed. For example, healthy human communities do not grow on worn-out soil. Further, we must be alive to those characteristics which distinguish us from other forms of life, so that our environment can be controlled in such a way as

The person who lives in constant awareness of Nature responds emotionally to it. As a participator, he understands, orders, and cherishes the natural world.

to give these precious human traits more scope, more chance to grow.

Our world to-day is a sympathetic one for this attitude of the participator, perhaps more so than it has been at any time since primitive living was left behind. In many ways we have learned to recognize our depredations, to restore resources and keep the balance equitable. The era of the mine is passing. Electricity, generated by water-power as the by-product of an intelligent handling of soil erosion and flood control, is coming more and more to be our major source of power. Industry is thus becoming linked to a force that is constructive instead of exploitative. The increasing use of agricultural products in industry is another step in this direction. Dispersal of power over transmission lines and the use of the automobile both help to spread us out. We do not need to live huddled together about one central source of water-power or steam. We can live in smaller groups, where nature has more room to show herself, and still carry on the work that needs to be done.

Our world can have a biotechnic civilization, as Lewis Mumford has aptly called it—a civilization that uses its technics for biological ends, the ends of richer functioning and sounder growth. But to realize this potentiality, each of us must have a real sense of participating, of belonging in this natural world. How, then, can we help children to become participators?

The person who feels himself genuinely a part of his natural surroundings seeks to understand what goes on around him. He is aware of his own interference, of the changes that his own presence necessarily brings about. Therefore he orders his natural environment consciously. Moreover, the person who lives in constant awareness of nature responds emotionally to it; he appreciates and enjoys the manifold beauty that surrounds him. Thus the participator is one who *understands, orders,* and *cherishes* the natural world. As parents, we have unique opportunities for helping children do all three of these things.

It may seem, at first glance, that adequate understanding, including as it does specific knowledge and an accumulation of facts, would come more properly within the province of a teacher than within that of a parent. But there is a close relation between understanding, ordering, and cherishing, that can often be achieved in the sustained life of the home better than in the school.

To understand, one must have an active share in the ordering that is man's adjustment to nature. This is sometimes possible in a school program, but family life gives even more opportunity for it. Moreover, that appreciation, that deeper perception which gives meaning to both understanding and ordering, and which we have called cherishing, grows best at home. It needs an intimate and sustained environment in order to flourish. A little child's emotional response to beauty begins to develop long before he goes to school. It is closely linked with personal relationships, with the perceptions and responses of those to whom he is emotionally tied.

In the daily round of intimate, busy living that goes on at home, therefore, we can help children develop a sense of belonging, of being a part of the natural world.

II

Helping Children Understand Their Natural Environment

UNDERSTANDING THE NATURAL WORLD HAS TWO SIDES. It includes a grasp of the underlying relationships that determine this world, as well as familiarity with the many living things that go to make it up. Familiarity with individuals, unless it is tempered with a concept that relates them to some more broadly comprehended whole, is not enough. Being able to recognize the broader concepts of natural law without having a warm, personal familiarity with individuals is not desirable, either. There must be understanding in both spheres. The underlying concepts form a frame of reference, a skeleton plan; familiarity with individuals and particulars provides the living flesh.

At whatever point a child touches the natural world, the immediate experience is only one link in an endless chain, only a small sector of the multiple pattern which extends fanwise and can be explored in every direction. Our part in this exploring is to provide opportunities for it and to try to be aware ourselves in what directions each single experience may lead. This may sound like a large order, but innumerable opportunities for linking specific experiences to underlying relationships turn up in the ordinary course of events if we are on the lookout for them. The following instances of ways in which such opportunities were used in a school situation may be suggestive.

Exploring the work of sunlight. We were raking up leaves in the play-yard. Suddenly Johnnie gave a shout: "Come and see what a funny thing I've found!" He was holding in his hand a thin, straggling plant, white from its burial under the leaves. All the children were interested. What made it look so queer? That its strangeness had something to do with its being covered was plain.

We took the yellowed leaves indoors with us when we went. Later, the subject was brought up once more. This plant had been in the dark. Did plants need light to be green? Perhaps they needed light to grow, for this one we had found in the dark certainly wasn't very healthy-looking; its stems were spindling and its leaves were stunted. Why did sunlight help plants to grow?

The ability of green leaves, in the presence of sunlight, to convert carbon dioxide and water into the carbohydrates that are necessary for both plants and animals as food is one of the keystones of our existence. Without this ability, there could be no world, natural or social, as we know it. Here was the chance to drive this all-important relationship home.

First we explored what made the white leaf different. A drop of iodine solution on the bleached leaf and on a green one (whose chlorophyl was first removed by immersion in alcohol, so that we could see our results better) showed a blue spot on the latter, but no blue color on the former. Next, this iodine test was tried on a piece of raw potato. Here, too, was the blue stain. Potatoes were "food." The green leaf, then, had "food" in it, too. But there was no "food" in the pale one.

To make the experiment more graphic still, we tried it out on one of our own potted plants. This was set in a dark closet for a day. Then we brought it out and covered one leaf entirely with tinfoil, leaving the other leaves exposed to strong sunlight. After about an hour the iodine test for starch was tried. Sure enough, the leaf that had been covered before exposure did not show any blue. Leaves need sunlight, then, we found, to manufacture food.

Exploring insect pollination. If Jane had not been stung, we might never have been launched on this voyage of exploration. But stings are uncomfortable, and one way of forgetting one's discomfort is to become very much interested in something else. So we went back to the honeysuckle bush, Jane and I, to find out why it was so popular with the bees. Being careful this time not to get in their way, we watched what they were doing. Other children joined us, and soon Richard announced that there were "crawly" insects on the flowers, too. What were they after, anyway?

An old trick of my childhood came back to me. Picking a few of the tiny trumpets, I suggested that the children taste the tapered ends. The sweetish nectar gave them the necessary clue. Then we explored the flowers themselves, the sticky stigmas and the anthers dusty with pollen. We watched a particularly clumsy bumblebee struggle to reach a flower's hoard. We saw him buzz off to another blossom and repeat his searchings. Agnes ran in for the small field lens that was always handy on a shelf, and we looked at several of the stigmas carefully, discovering some grains of pollen that had stuck.

The next day, when some one remarked that the bees were still busy, I thought we might go a bit further in our exploration. Choosing some blossoms that were not fully open, I suggested that we cover them with a paper bag so that the bees could not reach them. From others we carefully snipped the petal-tops, being careful not to injure the stamens that adhered to their base. Would the insects visit these "undressed" flowers, too? Our results may not have been controlled well enough for a scientific experiment, but they were clear enough to point the close connection between the honeysuckle blossoms and the bees, and to show what flower petals are for.

Exploring the needs of germination and growth. We had been talking a lot about the garden that we were finally going to have, space for it having been found after much thought. Space was at a premium, and I was not entirely sure that the reserving of even a tiny plot was warranted in such a small play-yard. The enthusiasm that greeted the idea, however, was answer enough. It was still too early to plant outdoors, but it occurred to me that some experiments with seeds indoors might be a worthwhile introduction as well as an immediate outlet for the newly aroused interest.

So one morning a cup of dried Lima beans was begged from the kitchen. It came as a new idea to most of the children that these were seeds. Their experience had been that seeds came in bright-colored packets with a picture of a flower on the outside. We laid out the beans in a shallow pan and covered them with water to soak overnight. Then we talked about what would be needed to start them growing. The response was prompt and unanimous. All we needed, according to every one, was "dirt."

So we started to explore. The next day we looked carefully at one of the soaked beans and discovered its stem and leaves in embryo. We also tried the iodine test for starch on its cotyledons and discovered that here was "food." I had prepared three small baking cups by putting wet blotting paper in the bottom of each. Into each one we put several beans. Labels on the side marked them 1 - 2 - 3.

During the next few days they sat together in a row on a shelf out of the bright light. But they were treated quite differently. The seeds in 1 were kept half-covered with water; the blotting paper in 2 was kept just moist; 3 we did not water at all after it was set away. Toward the end of the week the beans in 2 began to sprout; they had begun to grow. The other two cups were watched anxiously for a few more days. Then Andrew announced that we had better throw them out. They just weren't going to do anything. So we found that water was needed to make seeds sprout, but not too much water. We had begun a chart, to tell what we found out. This fact was added to the discovery that our seeds already had a supply of "food."

Next day the three cups were prepared again, and more seeds were put in them. This time, however, they were given the same amount of moisture but were set in different places. We asked Anna if we could put one on the shelf over the stove in the kitchen. Here it would be really warm. One we put back on the shelf where the others had been, and one we put outside the window. Once more a few days of waiting gave us results. Seeds must not be too hot, or too cold, to sprout.

While this last experiment was going on we were also trying something else. A wide-mouthed bottle was filled with moist sand and seeds were put into it, then the lid was screwed tight. We waited quite a while for these seeds to show sprouts, but they never did. They needed to "breathe"; they needed air to sprout.

The right amount of water and air, the right temperature, and some food—these, then, were what seeds needed in order to sprout. But now we were ready to watch one of our seedlings for a little longer. We made a seed-case by taping two small panes of window-glass to narrow strips of wood, so that we had two glass sides through which to watch the seedlings. Day by day we noticed how the root system developed downward and how the two little leaves began to push up. Soon the cotyledons shriveled and dried up; the leaves showed green. Now, we knew, with the help of the sun the seedlings were ready to manufacture their own food.

Using other seeds, we explored further. Flats, prepared

with different soil materials, were sprinkled with a quick-growing grass seed. In one we put sand; in another, peat-moss and sand; in two others, the traditional mixture of one-third sand, one-third peat-moss, one-third soil. The results showed us clearly that more was needed to make plants keep on growing than to start them off. All the flats sprouted, but only the last two really grew thickly. By adding fertilizer to one of these, the differences in soil mixtures and their effect on growth also became part of the picture.

By the time it was warm enough (and now we knew that seeds needed a warm—but not too warm—temperature) to plant outdoors, we had come to be curious about how our seeds would fare there. We could keep them moist, and we knew they would have air. But we also knew that later, when they were started, they would also need a good soil. What kind of soil did we have? And what made a good soil?

We brought a spadeful of dirt indoors and tried to find of what it was composed. We went exploring outdoors, too. We noticed the difference in vegetation between the road-cut near us and the woods that were several miles away. We brought back a little dirt from each. By washing these through, we could tell something about how they differed. The spadeful from the garden had sand in it, for the tiny grains could be seen. There was also something that made the water cloudy when it was shaken up. But this garden soil was mostly made up of "mud," as the children called it. In the spadeful from the woods there was "mud," too. Besides, there were lots of little pieces of things—twigs, parts of leaves, some bits of insect shell. We could not see many sand grains, and the water did not get so cloudy, either. As for the spadeful from the bank, it did not contain much that floated, like the pieces of twigs and leaves that came from the woods; but the water took a long time to settle, and when we left what was at the bottom to dry, it grew hard and cracked. Even Murray, who wasn't very interested and had not helped us much, noticed its similarity to the clay that we kept on the closet shelf.

Further explorations showed us top-soil in the making. The near-by truck-farmer showed us his compost heap, where organic refuse decayed into fertilizer. The children were quick to see the similarity between the disintegration that took place here and that which was taking place naturally in the woods. We brought back leaf-mold to be spaded into the garden. The next step, however, we did not take. No one raised the question of what caused the disintegration, and I knew a microscopic view would not mean very much to six-year-olds. The fact that dead things decay was left, for the time being, a fact without a "why." The cycle itself, however, was clear.

Exploring the work of water. These explorations occurred off and on for several months. The necessity for better drainage in the play-yard started them. After one heavy rain, the rivulets that made small gullies in our clay soil were particularly noticeable. This was in the autumn, and where the fallen leaves caught in the sparse grass, they formed a barrier which stopped the washing away of the soil. In one place, on a hard surface that had no vegetation, a sticky pool was formed; just beyond, where our garden had been, the water soaked into the friable soil as into a sponge.

We noticed all these things. Not far from us a new highway cut showed some of them on a larger scale. One of its banks was seamed with gullies. Farther on the WPA men were planting small shrubs to hold the soil. This performance interested Andrew especially.

"Why, that's what they did at the beach," he remarked. "Is the wind going to blow the sand away here, too?"

We picked up some of the clayey soil and decided it didn't feel like sand. Here it was clear that wind and water both have an effect upon the land. It was also clear how important are the roots of plants.

These discoveries made their impression, too. Several months later, when we were trying to decide where to set out some plants that had been started indoors, Richard suggested that we put them "where the rain makes a path, the way the road men do." As an experiment, we put some of them there, and when the next rain washed them out, a lively discussion ensued. We decided to try grass sod, instead of tender seedlings, to stop the paths of the rain.

During the winter we seized the opportunity of exploring the states of water and their relation to temperature. Snow was brought in and melted. Then the same pan of water was set on an electric plate and heated. The shiny side of an aluminum pot served to show the condensation of the steam. Some of the water was then put into a small test-tube and set outside the window to stay overnight. In the morning its cracked sides showed clearly what the expanding force of freezing water can do.

A window-pane steamed by a sudden drop in temperature interested us, too, and the aluminum pot was drawn into service again. This time we filled it with water of room temperature and cooled it by adding ice, noticing the point at which its sides became clouded. Water was always in the air, then, even though we didn't always see it. This led to some talk about rain and the changes of temperature outside. The next day we set up a crude but effective barometer. Using two room thermometers, I wrapped the bulb of one in a piece of wet cheese-cloth, leaving one end of the cloth in a cup of water so that it would keep constantly wet. When it came time to wash up, I drew the children's attention to something they had never consciously remarked before, so far as I knew: that if you do not wipe your hands on a towel, but let them dry in the air, they feel colder. As the water evaporated from the wet-bulb thermometer, it would get colder, too, and the line of mercury would drop. So we could tell how much moisture there was in the air, even though we couldn't see it, by looking at the two thermometers. For a few weeks we read our thermometers every day, making predictions about the weather, some of which were right and some of which were not. But the venture served to keep in our minds the fact that there is always water in the air.

Our interest in the garden led to an exploration of the work of water in another way. The fact that seeds must be kept moist had been accepted, after the first experiments with the Lima beans, without further curiosity. It was only later, when a dressing of bone-meal had been put around some young plants, that some one asked how it would "get inside." This seemed a good chance to explore the work of water as a solvent and carrier. Every one knew, of course, that many things dissolve in water, but this commonplace had never before been connected with other observations. Now we really investigated, trying out a number of things to see whether they would or would not dissolve. The fact that water is evaporated from the surface of leaves was then made evident by covering with a jelly-glass one of our potted plants that had recently been watered and noticing the drops of moisture that formed, after a time, on the glass. Water could carry the things that plants needed, then, on its journey from roots to leaves.

Keeping track of the sun. We began to to talk in January about having a garden. Some one asked how long it would be before we could begin. I said that the sun would have to be a lot nearer than it was then, before it would be warm enough for things to grow. After that, we began to watch the sun. That day, at noon, we noticed the shadow of our jungle gym. By experimenting indoors with shadows, we found out that the higher the source of light is, the shorter the shadow; also that the direction of a shadow changes with a shift in the position of the light.

Picking out one of the jungle-gym poles to watch, we marked the position of its shadow the next day at noon, and every week the marker was corrected to the new position. We could see that the shadow was becoming shorter and that it was shifting, too.

One day, at lunch, we got interested in where the carrots we were eating came from. Some one remarked that it must be a place where the sun was already warm. After that I checked with the daily market report once in a while, and we marked with thumb-tacks on a large map the states that were supplying our table with the things we couldn't yet grow ourselves. As spring approached, therefore, we knew it in two ways—by our shadow in the yard and by the line of thumb-tacks that showed on the map. By the time we were eating the harvest of lettuce from Virginia, we ourselves were putting in lettuce seed.

In these explorations, growing out of immediate experiences, we gave meaning to the fundamental relationships that underlie everyday living. By consciously thinking about them and connecting them, we recognized their place in a related scheme. Water was no longer merely something that came out of the faucet; it was an ever-present necessity whose work in the world we recognized and appreciated. We also knew its destructiveness and realized our own part in controlling this. When the muddy puddle in the play-yard was a nuisance, Andrew remarked, "If we hadn't walked there so much, the water wouldn't stand on top; it would go in!" So it was with other things. After we visited our neighbor, the truck-farmer, some one wanted to know why we couldn't have a compost heap, too—"Anna has lots of good fertilizer in the kitchen!"

Once a few fundamental relationships such as these are recognized and thought about, there is no limit to the number of observations that take on new meaning. Every auto trip, every vacation, is grist to one's mill. The seashore offers many chances for seeing the work of wind and water at first hand. The mountains may offer a first-hand study of a balanced environment, where plant and animal life has found an equilibrium of optimum growth; or it may show only too dramatically the devastating effects of uncontrolled interference.

Even the limited area that a young child can cover on his own offers him a wealth of material for tracing out connections. The kinds of plants that grow in shaded woods differ from those that grow in sunny pastures; one can discover how plants are fitted for the places in which they grow. In every back yard there are enough small lives to point out the myriad relationships between plants and animals. Everywhere the earth is changing, and every few feet of ground bears evidence of this for all to read. The pattern is endless. All one needs, to trace it, is a seeing eye and the habit of looking for the other end of the thread.

Becoming familiar with individuals. The natural world is a place where children are constantly making new acquaintances and meeting old friends. An ability to call one's friends by name is a help toward this kind of familiarity. If one does not know their names, it is well to be able to tell in a more general way who they are, to what family or related group they belong. Scientific classification is a complicated matter, often based on structural differences that are not readily apparent. However, there are easily noted details which indicate kinship among many of the individuals in both the plant and the animal kingdoms.

Certain groups of individuals become better known, or known in more detail, because they live closer to us. Others become so because they are especially interesting in behavior or appearance. A child may know a number of flowers by name and be able to place many more in their respective families by recognizing family characteristics; yet a fern or a mushroom may remain merely a fern or a mushroom and be quite sufficiently named for him. He may know many different birds by name, recognizing both their species and their family group; yet fishes or frogs may not be particularized at all.

Although the immediate environment makes a difference in what groups are chosen for particular naming (children at the seashore will get acquainted with groups of marine invertebrates entirely unknown to the inland child), there are certain groups, in both the animal and the vegetable kingdom, which are especially useful for this purpose. Through familiarity with them, and an ability to place new finds in the proper classification within their bounds, children very soon become aware that all living things have likenesses and differences which show relatedness. Insects, plants with conspicuous flowers, small mammals, and birds are such convenient groupings. Each one contains

Just looking at "trees" and "flowers" is not at all the same thing as seeing them with the discriminating eye that notes their differences as well as their similarities.

families whose individuals are easily recognizable, and each one supplies ample scope for specific identification.

If we are interested in stressing relationships as well as naming individuals, it is not enough to know that an ant is an ant or that a beetle is a beetle. The fact that they both have jointed bodies and six legs is also important. It distinguishes them from the earthworm, whose body is not jointed, and the spider, who boasts eight legs. If one can tell a daisy or a wild mustard flower, one can also recognize the kinship of cone-flower, aster, or (on closer inspection) goldenrod to the former; can link arabis, alyssum, and cress by the similarity of their cross-shaped petal arrangement with the latter. The sparrows, the warblers, the flycatchers, all have characteristic manners that in each case mark their numerous species as kin. One might not be sure of the exact identity of the new-comer but could never take him for a sparrow if he belonged to the warbler tribe.

The ability to identify also serves another purpose. It opens up new fields of interest by splitting up well-known general groups into a number of unknown but much more interesting individuals. Just looking at "trees" or "flowers" is not at all the same thing as seeing them with the discriminating eye that notes their differences as well as their similarities. To discover the first is just as thrilling as to recognize the second. For the person whose trees are birch and beech and oak (better still, pin oak, chestnut oak, etc.), the woods become a friendlier and more interesting place to be.

We can foster an interest in identification in several ways.

By naming the familiar creatures and plants roundabout ourselves, we start the ball rolling. If all things that crawl are "bugs" and all things we have not planted in the garden are "weeds," there is little incentive actually to look at them, to know them for what they are. If, on the other hand, the usual garden inhabitants are named and known, a new arrival will inevitably be an object of interest and curiosity. The habit of recognizing the living things about us, and of being curious as to the ones we do not know, can be begun almost as soon as we start to explore the world at all. Once begun, it is a habit that is sure to grow.

As children grow older they can be encouraged to use reference material for finding out what they want to know. A shelf of reference books deserves a place in every home library. At first the language of these texts may be hard to understand, and help will be needed in using them. One family used a flower identification book of this kind from the start, and while Father did the looking up at first, every one else helped out. The date and place of each find were carefully noted in the margin. Now a grown-up family still uses the same book, and the records in the margin show a continuity of well over twenty years. Growing into one's tools in this way has its advantages. It makes experience all of a piece. There are other aids to identification that are good standard home equipment, too: a pair of field-glasses and a handy field-microscope. Both of these can be secured in models that are reasonably priced and durable. A camera is also a help.

In any detailed identification, a collection of specimens

is useful. Flowers and leaves are particularly adapted to simple collecting. A flower-press can be made by nailing thin strips of wood in lattice fashion to make two squares about fourteen by fourteen inches. An old trunk or suitcase strap can be used to belt these together. The flowers one wishes to press are spread out between newspapers, several thicknesses between every two flowers. Blotting-paper is laid on top and bottom. Then the whole is put between the wooden lattice squares and tightly strapped. Pressed flowers can be mounted on heavy manila paper, each sheet telling when and where the plant was found, in addition to its name. The use of a camera can make such a collection even more interesting, for pictures give one a record of habitat as well. Pictures also supplement a collection of tree leaves, for the pressed leaves can be accompanied by a picture that shows the general shape of a tree and by one that shows in a closer view the appearance of its bark.

III

Helping Children Order Their Natural Environment

THE COLLECTIONS WE MAKE TO HELP IN NAMING AND placing individuals are an ordering of nature, an artificial setting up of conditions for the purpose of better understanding. The experiments described in the preceding pages are also an ordering of this kind. Collecting and experimenting are both valuable tools for rounding out experience with more detailed and accurate knowledge. They are, however, only tools—means to an end, not ends in themselves.

When children become interested in collecting objects, therefore, the collections should mean something. Dead butterflies, fertilized birds' eggs, even a pressed pasture rose are legitimate toll only if they are to be of some use. Properly stored and labeled, they can be valuable as reference and for purposes of comparison. Collecting just to collect does not foster a sense of the worth of these things in and for themselves.

In order to serve a child's best purposes, experimenting also must be undertaken with some definite end in view. It must be firmly linked to past experience and must logically lead a step further. The use of scientific equipment (a chemical set, for instance) to produce wonders, or to amuse as a toy, is not experimenting in this sense. Using the same set to test the soil in one's garden, with a previous knowledge of what growing things need and with the intention of making the soil conform more nearly to this ideal growing medium, would be genuine experimenting. In using the wealth of material that is so readily available, one must be careful that experimenting remains sincere and purposeful.

In an essay in her *Common Reader* on the seventeenth-century gentleman-naturalist, John Evelyn, Virginia Woolf has this to say:

"But as for going into the house to fetch a knife and with that knife dissecting a Red Admiral's [butterfly's] head, as Evelyn would have done, no sane person in the twentieth century would entertain such a project for a second. Individually, we may know as little as Evelyn, but collectively we know so much that there is little incentive to venture on private discoveries. We seek the encyclopedia, not the scissors; and know in two minutes not only more than was known to Evelyn in his life-time, but that the mass of knowledge is so vast that it is scarcely worthwhile to possess a single crumb." *

Yet an "incentive to venture on private discoveries" is a rather satisfying asset. Unless one has the alert eye and inquiring mind that go with a use of the scissors, encyclopedias are not of much use. Knowledge can be acquired

* Virginia Woolf, *The Common Reader* (New York, Harcourt, Brace and Company, 1929), pp. 111-22.

only by a wise portioning of both scissors and encyclopedia —beginning at the scissors end.

The youngster who looks at what he sees and tries to find out something about it by himself before he is even aware that his answers can be found in books has an advantage that will always stand him in good stead. It does not greatly matter that his discoveries have probably all been made and their implications acted upon by other people. They will still be significant discoveries for him. He will still get the thrill of finding out something for himself. The oftener we can parry a question with the invitation "Let's see if we can find out," the better. In this way even the commonplaces are a challenge, and therefore interesting.

We order the natural world for other reasons than to understand it. We order to improve, to enjoy, and to live. Children can have a share in all these. A well-rounded gardening experience assures them this, for the gardener does all three of these things: He improves plant growth by selecting his breeds, by fertilizing, and by cultivation. He plans his garden so that it will be pleasing to the eye, a landscape to enjoy. He grows and nurtures plants for the food they provide.

The opportunities of a gardening experience. Even though we are living, most of us, three times removed from the soil that feeds us, it is a valuable part of every child's experience to have some direct contact with it, no matter how small. A crop of radishes grown in a window-box, if that is all that can be managed, is worth seeing through.

Some space that is his, about which he can say, "This is my garden," is by far the best plan.

When there is space outdoors for a garden, the opportunities are many. In order to have meaning for him, however, a child's gardening experience must be a satisfying one. Just helping with garden chores does not give him enough scope nor provide him with enough interest. Some space that is his, for which he takes full responsibility and about which he can say, "This is *my* garden," is by far the best plan.

Even a little child can have such a plot and from it make his contribution to the family table, whether this contribution be decoration or food. The lettuce that the five-year-old grows himself takes on added flavor in the eating if it is enjoyed by the rest of the family, too. The first cutting of pansies from one's own garden space looks more beautiful than ever on the dining-room table or as a bouquet picked especially to honor a family guest. Gardening is valuable for its first-hand contacts with growing things; but it is valuable for its social contributions, too. A satisfying gardening experience provides for both.

Here are a few suggestions for gardens that make these provisions. They can be undertaken by children of six or seven, in a small space, yet they present a real job that is worth doing.

A cutting garden. There are many annuals that are easily grown for indoor bouquets and that are colorful and interesting to grow. Nasturtiums, marigolds, zinnias, phlox, calendulas, snapdragons, and asters are all good for this purpose. Seed catalogues carry ample cultural directions.

A salad garden. If the home plot is not big enough to support a vegetable garden, a salad garden can be very useful to the family kitchen. In it can be grown the vegetables that are habitually eaten raw: lettuce, carrots, radishes, onions, chives, and parsley; a few plants each of peppers and cauliflower; a few cabbage heads, cucumbers, and tomatoes if space permits. The seed catalogue will tell which of these can be readily raised from seed and which are best bought as plants.

An herb garden. The small aromatic plants that make cooking a piquant affair can be provided by the young gardener in limited space. Chives, parsley, thyme, summer savory, marjoram, basil, and tarragon make a useful combination. Little green bouquets of these can be cut to go into stews and soups. They can also be dried for winter use. They add flavor to the salad bowl and to the picnic sandwich. Here again the seed catalogue is helpful with cultural directions.

A "preserving" crop. If there is enough space to grow a surplus crop that can be used during the winter, garden experience can be broadened still further. The forethought made necessary by seasonal changes is an important part of our ordering of nature. The fact that we often do it now by planting in different places, following the sun, does not make it any the less important as a necessity, only more remote. A surplus crop kept for winter use makes this necessity directly apparent.

An extra pepper plant will yield peppers for pickling

or for using in a relish; two or three tomato plants should yield enough tomatoes for at least a pint jar of soup or juice; an extra row of carrots or radishes can be stored in sand and kept in a cool place until later in the season, when fresh ones are all gone. One family used these small surpluses at the holiday meals later in the year. A plate of tomato soup that was made out of Richard's own tomatoes proved a particularly satisfying introduction to dinner on Thanksgiving Day.

Other opportunities for ordering. The young gardener has still other opportunities for arranging, for ordering, the natural environment. All gardeners soon discover how important birds are. Attracting birds to one's garden can be an interesting venture in itself and will be repaid in better crops as well as in enjoyment. A bird bath can be planned to make a decorative feature in a small garden plot. Nesting boxes set up in the shrubbery or in trees that are not too close also serve two purposes: they invite birds to keep our garden free of troublesome insects, and they bring bird families close enough for us to watch. By letting some of our annual flowers go to seed, we can supply additional bird food as well. Many birds are particularly fond of the seeds of sunflowers, portulaca, asters, and zinnias. A few shrubs, planted especially with bird tastes in mind, are also an invitation. Once I counted fifteen different species of birds on a wild cherry bush in the corner of a vegetable garden. When the "tomato worms" appeared, we had particular reason to be thankful for that wild cherry bush, for many of these birds were quite ready to take to the caterpillars, too. Many birds are fond of the berries of viburnum, honeysuckle, and dogwood. One or more of these can be planted with bird neighbors in mind.

Other creatures, too, are useful in a garden. The large web of the garden spider, tucked away among the flowers, will catch many insects that might do much harm. Toads are also a help. Earthworms do good work in the soil. Young gardeners can learn to recognize the value of these inhabitants and make some provisions for them, at least to the extent of letting them alone.

Many of the creatures one finds in gardens are interesting in themselves. They deserve to be better known. If there is a place where they may be temporarily housed, their ways will be easier to watch. An old aquarium that is set up as a miniature piece of the outdoors can be used to accommodate such finds temporarily. If it is planted with a number of the common weeds and kept moist, almost all insects can be kept long enough to see how they really look and act. Here one can see what happens to the "cabbage worm" after he has had his fill of cabbage; how ants go about making a place for themselves; what will come out of the egg-mass or cocoon that has been found among the flowers. If any creatures are to be permanent residents, their food supply will, of course, have to be replenished.

IV

Helping Children Cherish Their Natural Environment

CHERISHING THE WORLD OF NATURE IS ESSENTIALLY AN artist's approach. The scientist seeks to understand, to name and place and know. The gardener orders. But it is the artist who appreciates with no other purpose in view and, in an effort to objectify that appreciation, re-creates. The true participator has this appreciation as a valuable ingredient in all his contacts. He is a naturalist as well as a scientist. His gardening is esthetic as well as utilitarian. But there are times when the artist comes to the fore, when the glow of the western sky or the patterned design of bare tree branches requires only an esthetic response. It is important for us, as parents, to give the scientist scope, to give the gardener opportunities. It is important for us to recognize the artist in our children, too.

Developing a sensitivity to natural beauty. Esthetic appreciation has two elements. There is, first of all, a sensitivity to beauty, to the pleasing arrangement of color and line. One does not need to know many small children, to be convinced that a feel for design and color is part of their innate equipment. This is not surprising when one thinks it through. Our own bodies are made on a symmetrical plan. Design, or pattern, occurs in many forms in both inanimate and animate nature. The circle, the curve, the spiral, to mention only a few design elements, are repeated again and again. Even the tiny pattern on the body of a flower-fly is meticulously and beautifully balanced. No wonder, then, that these forms, and an innate sense of symmetry, of balance, should be part of our heritage; no wonder that a sweeping curve or a nicely balanced arrangement of angles gives us pleasure. We like what we are used to, and nature has made us abundantly used to her beauty of pattern and line.

Innate sensibilities, however, must have a chance to develop. Children may delight in natural beauty long before they are consciously aware of the sources of their pleasure. If we want them to retain a sensitive awareness of, and delight in, the beauty of natural things, we ourselves must feel that awareness and delight. For the little child's first response is pure well-being. He does not know why the sunny day, the smell of flowers, the green of trees make him feel good. It is our companionship, our participation, that help him to a more conscious enjoyment of these things.

To the discerning eye, beauty is abundant. Even above a crowded city street there are clouds, and the full moon occasionally stands framed in an apartment window. But there must be time to enjoy, time to watch while the spider spins her web or the colors glow and shift and fade within a cloud bank. We are forced to crowd our lives with

*Plants give perhaps the most easily observed variety of design ...
constantly offering new and pleasing patterns.*

so many things, with so much clutter, that we often lose the habit of enjoying. We do not take the time to admire the pattern of a vanessa moth's wings or the crystal shapes of frost upon the window-pane. We do not take the time to look, and passing these things by, we come to take them for granted. As penalty, we lose the power of seeing.

This is what we must guard against, both for ourselves and for our children. Valuable time does not need to be crowded with happenings. The supposedly empty minutes can be filled with the most precious freight of all. What if it is time to go calling or to do the morning's shopping? If Peter is intrigued with the frost flowers on the window or with the drops of rain that sparkle tiny rainbows on a bush outside, it is worth while stopping long enough to enjoy these with him, to discover new frost patterns, brighter raindrop colors, together.

Plants give perhaps the most easily observed variety of design. The arrangements of stamens, pistils, sepals, and petals; the flowering umbel, spike, or composite head; the pattern of a seed-pod or the curved grace of ballasted seeds—these are constantly offering new and pleasing patterns. Sometimes the most unexpected places yield the most interesting finds, and this is itself cause for delight. Seven-year-old Faith was trying out a newly acquired field-glass, applying its magnification indiscriminately to the growing things just beyond the porch steps. Suddenly she called, "Aunt Mary, look! Look what I've found! Who'd have guessed this was a pretty one!" Her glass had revealed the meticulously beautiful arrangement of a tiny chickweed flower, a blossom so insignificant that, although common enough to be an unwelcome weed in the garden, its intrinsic beauty had never been remarked before.

By being quick to appreciate a child's discoveries, we can help him develop a discerning eye. If Aunt Mary had been too occupied to come and see, or if she had disregarded Faith's interest, interrupting her with a new demand, the child might well have forgotten all about her new find. After all, this is so much an adult world, even for children. What is important to adults becomes important to them, too. Disregarding the chickweed flower would have done a lot to make it of no account.

Watching for the beauty in things also helps to widen boundaries in another way. Because of our own unfortunate first contacts, we are likely to pass on attitudes of disgust or fear to children. An earthworm, because of his sliminess, may seem a disgusting thing. But if one takes the time to watch him move across the sidewalk, the ripple of his muscles, which is his way of getting places, is a beautiful thing to see. The discarded shell of a cicada may be a fearful object to a child because it is strange. Holding it to the light and noticing the iridescence of the chitin invests it with beauty and interest.

The natural environment is peculiarly endowed to keep senses alert, to sharpen sensibilities. In our man-made world the stimuli are too incessant and too strident. We become immune to sound, to movement, even to form and color. There are too many things to hear and see. In self-defense, nerve-endings become dulled, insensitive. The city-dweller realizes this when he stays for a while in the country, when he frequents the fields, the woods, or the hilly pasturelands. It is not only that the pressure of environment is lessened—the weight of noise, of rush, and of responsibility; after a time there comes a purely sensual satisfaction in allowing each faculty full play. The few sounds stretch the sense of hearing; each movement that catches the eye has significance; forms stand out as meaningful; gradations of color, shifts of light and shade, challenge perception. These subtle appeals are restful. Attending to them is a valuable exercise in relaxation. We are giving children a useful defense against later tenseness, then, when we help them to develop a sensitive awareness to natural beauty.

Wondering is a part of esthetic appreciation. Do other animals wonder? We do not know. But surely our own most precious possession is this second ingredient of esthetic appreciation, intangible though it is. From it has sprung the idealism that shapes the gods. It touches the depths of our emotional drives. From it springs curiosity, the urge to know and understand. But wonder itself is not intellectual. It is too fundamental for that. It is the impetus, the leaven. Without it there would be no curiosity and consequently no knowing. There would be no truly esthetic appreciation, either. Wonder underlies them both.

The slow growth of a tree root that splits the rocky ledge; the sprouting of grass-blades in the mud lining of a swallow's nest; the fury of the wind that bends and breaks a tree—these are all displays of energy, of power. They are just cause for wondering.

The little boy who wakes at night to see a myriad of

tiny, twinkling stars or the far-off shining of the moon is moved by an inarticulate emotion which is a wonder of immensities, of the vastness of space that is to him the sky.

The manifold interrelations that exist in nature, their intricacy and infinite variety, also inspire this feeling. No matter how much we can anticipate, how much we may come to know about these things, there is always a margin of unbelievableness, of mystery, left. This excites our wonder and is the basis for our reverence.

Just as there must be time to admire, so there must be time for wondering. It is the product of outwardly idle minutes, of periods of quiet and rest. It is the product of solitude, but companionship is an essential part of it, too. Sharing these experiences of awe and reverence, of wonder, with those we love strengthens and supports not only reverence, but love. Here we come to the heart of the reason why an attitude toward the natural world is best developed within a family. The blending of reverence and love that results when parents and children share their experiences of wonder is a sure base for understanding and ordering—a base that is not so surely formed in any other way.

Making opportunities for re-creation. We have said that cherishing is an artist's approach to nature and that the artist re-creates. Passive enjoyment, therefore, is only half a response. Re-creation of some sort is also part of this experience. It is the artist that goes all the way. For the little child this may be only the spontaneous expression in words of a new delight, nothing more than a long-drawn "O-o-oh! *So* soft!" at the downy feeling of a baby chicken's feathers. But such spontaneity is the beginning of the artist's re-creation, an attempt to articulate in some way what one feels.

We can encourage the use of words to describe the look and feeling of things by making opportunities for it and by giving the best of it some permanent form. As children grow older they can be encouraged to make such records of experience themselves. The record of a field trip does not need to be only a tabulation of data and finds. The surroundings of a rocky hillside where the columbine was discovered, how the world looked and felt on that sunny spring day, are worth recounting, too.

Sometimes the way other people have described such experiences is an incentive and a help to re-creation of this kind. One youngster used the expression, "I heard the stillness all around," in describing a visit to the woods. Keats' "little noiseless noise among the leaves" and Dorothy Wordsworth's "that noiseless noise that lives in the summer air" were interesting to him as indication that other people also had been aware of the vital quality of stillness he had been trying to describe. The knowledge that experiences of this kind are common to all people, to those who lived long ago as well as to one's self, has its value. It emphasizes in an intimate, understandable way the continuity that underlies our individual lives.

Children can use other mediums besides words in their re-creation. Sculpture materials such as clay and plasticene are useful, as are also the graphic ones of crayons and paint. Making pictures to illustrate a trip to the woods or the seashore helps to clarify the experience as well as to record it. Attempting to model a pet turtle or frog not only makes one more conscious of its anatomy, but makes its essential individuality more vivid. Older children can use a camera for the same purpose. Learning to frame a landscape or a group of near-by objects so that their entity is truly expressed is genuine re-creation. The photographer may achieve as much in this way as the painter or graphic artist if he understands his instrument and has a seeing eye.

Scientist, gardener, artist—children can, in some measure, be all three. The natural world is theirs to understand, to order, and to cherish. If we do our share by providing opportunities and by lending a sympathetic helping hand, our democracy may be a more beautiful, more friendly, more comfortable place in which to live. A sound adjustment to one's natural environment is by no means the whole answer, but it is a good beginning.

III

The Outside World of Machinery

I

The World of the Machine

"THE NATURE THAT DAWNS UPON THE MODERN CHILD IS one of myriad machines; the moral and esthetic universe which he constructs for himself comes to him as the spawn of myriad machines. If he is reared on a farm, motor, telephone, radio, and word and picture of the press are as natural to him as tree or cow. And, of course, the nature of the city is mechanical altogether. . . . Nature for the American is this iron chaos of life-providing, death-dealing, value-distilling forces." *

Of course, there is an exaggeration here. Even the city has its rain, its sky, its clouds, its birds; even, on occasion, its insect pests. Yet the world of the machine is without doubt a very important part of our lives. To many of us it is far more consciously an environment than is the underlying natural world, and its effects upon the way we live are far more spectacular. Certainly it merits equal consideration with the world of nature as a distinct environment, for its influence is fully as important in the establishing of basic attitudes. Moreover, the problems it raises are

* Waldo Frank, *The Rediscovery of America* (New York, Charles Scribner's Sons, 1929), p. 72.

likely to be much more acute and more immediately perplexing.

Before exploring these basic attitudes that are affected by machinery, however, it may be well to explore somewhat the mechanical environment in which we find ourselves. What is it like, this world of the machine?

Although machinery was used for purposes of manufacture before the eighteenth century (silk was spun by machinery in the fourteenth; knitting machines were invented in the sixteenth), it was not until that time that the introduction of coal as a source of mechanical power, the use of the steam engine to convert that power, and more effective methods of smelting and processing iron so speeded up the use of machinery that the resulting changes seriously upset a manageable balance. To quote Lewis Mumford:

"During this period [the seventeenth century] the machine was adequately complemented by the utility: if the watermill made more power available, the dyke and the drainage ditch created more usable soil. If the canal aided transport, the new cities aided social intercourse. In every department of activity there was equilibrium between the static and the dynamic, between the rural and the urban, between the vital and the mechanical." *

But the steam engine changed all this. It required a large investment of capital and it could only be run efficiently in large units and on a continuous schedule. Con-

* *Technics and Civilization* (New York, Harcourt, Brace and Company, 1934), p. 148.

centration of machinery into large plants; concentration of population about these plants; long hours of work; increasing specialization; multiplicity of products—these were the inevitable results. The machine age, as we know it, grew apace.

The most conspicuous feature of our industrial civilization, perhaps, is the rapidity with which it changes. The introduction of one new technic, or one new machine, often has far-reaching results. It may affect our lives in many unforeseen and unpredictable ways. One example shows this in striking fashion:

In the Middletown of the Lynds' study,* the first automobile appeared in 1900. An estimate of the number of automobiles in the area (including both city and county) six years later put it at two hundred; at the close of 1923 there were, roughly, two autos for every three families in the city alone. All phases of living were affected. Automobiles spread the holiday trip habit and consequently depleted Fourth of July parades and community picnics. The automobile was found to be a chief bond of interest between husband and wife, as well as a common cause of disagreement between parents and children of high-school age. The make of one's car rivaled the appearance of one's home plot as a sign of social prestige. Adolescents, especially, rated each other's social standing in terms of the family car. Local seedsmen attributed a decline in backyard gardening to the automobile, and local clothing mer-

* Robert S. and Helen Merrill Lynd, *Middletown: A Study in Contemporary American Culture* (New York, Harcourt, Brace and Company, 1929).

chants laid a falling-off of sales to its rival claims on the family budget. Factories drew on wider areas for their workmen, putting local labor at a new disadvantage. Sunday drives cut into church attendance. A local juvenile-court judge described the auto as a "house of prostitution on wheels." Thus, in the short space of twenty-three years, a new method of transportation, a new family necessity, and a new social and community problem grew from novelty to commonplace.

This rapidity of change in custom, in habits, even in values, which characterizes a widespread use of machinery, has made its assimilation difficult and extremely spotty. What, exactly, is meant by assimilation in this connection? In order to answer that question, we will have to go further back and ask another one. What, precisely, is a machine?

Machinery is such a common factor in our lives that we have all but forgotten the answer to that question. Men have always known that if they loosened their grasp upon an object, it would fall. The fact of gravity was so commonplace an experience that it took the genius of a Newton to be objective enough about it to pose a why and find the answer. To the children of an industrial age, the machine is pretty much the same kind of commonplace.

Machines as tools. A machine, no matter how complex its mechanism or how seemingly independent its operation, is a *tool*. It is either an extension of one of our five senses, making sight or hearing more acute, touch more sensitive; or it is a device for producing more energy, or for making energy go further, than is possible when our own bodies are its generating plant.

If we think of machines as tools, it is easier to estimate how well they have been assimilated. For a tool is something that is utilized for a given purpose in a given situation. A saw, for instance, is used by the man who finds that he needs two pieces of wood when he has only one piece. It is replaced by another tool, the hammer, when he has the two pieces of wood and wishes to join them together to form a differently shaped whole. He does not saw pieces of wood which he will not use, nor does he use the hammer just to make a noise or to see the nail go in. He uses each of these tools for a definite purpose. So far as he is concerned, they are assimilated.

The four-year-old child whose father owns these tools, however, will handle them quite differently. To him, the process of sawing, the back and forth motion of his arm, the falling off of the piece of wood, the sense of power that his ability to sever it gives, will be sufficient reason for using it. The four-year-old has not assimilated these tools. There is no particular reason why he should. His use of them serves the biological needs of a young child.

We use many of our machines as the four-year-old youngster uses the saw or the hammer. We become intrigued with what they will do. The speed of the auto, the distance obtainable on a radio, the incredible efficiency of the factory machine, sometimes seem more important to us than the uses for which they were designed.

When the Lynds returned to Middletown in 1935 * to evaluate the changes which five years of boom and five years of depression had brought about, they found that of all the retail trades and services which supply Middletown citizens, the only ones which could report no falling-off in business during the worst part of the depression were the filling-stations. Families whose wage-earners had been unemployed for some time, whose homes were mortgaged, and who were sometimes without adequate food and clothing still owned, and drove, their cars.

The automobile meant many things besides being a way of getting somewhere. It meant escape from accusing looks, from crowded streets, from troubling thoughts. It was a means of putting on a bold front to the neighborhood. It meant, for the driver sitting at the wheel of his car, at least an illusion of power and of self-respect. These are unassimilated uses, uses extraneous to the purpose of this particular tool. The needs thus answered are as much a part of human life as getting work done. What concerns us here is whether this tendency toward irrelevant use of machinery carries social consequences of any importance.

Results of an unassimilated use of machines. With profits as a motive, and propaganda a means, those who own the machines of the factories often deliberately take advantage of our lack of assimilation. We buy many machines, and many products of machinery, not because we

* *Middletown in Transition* (New York, Harcourt, Brace and Company, 1937).

need them or because they contribute anything worth-
while to our living but because we have been skilfully
manipulated toward that end. Such manipulation would
not be possible if we were using completely assimilated
tools. The man who needs a saw in order to make a set
of shelves for his wife's kitchen goes out and buys one
that will suit his purpose. He is not likely to buy a saw
just because his neighbor next door has one, or because
the picture and legend of the advertisement make him
feel ashamed that he does not own one, too.

To any one who watches the operation of machinery in
a modern industrial plant, a definition of the machine as a
tool may well seem almost fantastic. For to such an observer the tables seem reversed. On an assembly line it is
the man who is, to all intents and purposes, the tool. The
machine determines the pattern of his product and sets
the pace of his work. But the men on the assembly line
are the apparent tools of the machine only because, and
to the extent that, they are the tools of other men. It is
easy to see how this calculated use of both men and machinery came about. The profits which accrued from mass-
production at its beginning gave the machines of the
factory a distinct advantage over the men who worked
them. For it was the machine, not the man, who made
this mass-production possible. Another factor further em-
phasized this advantage. The purchase of machinery
necessitates a considerable financial outlay. Once installed,
it has to be kept running in order to continue to pay for
itself. Therefore, it is the more easily procured and re-

placed human element that is often sacrificed to the machine.

As consumers of the products of the factory machines, we are at least partly responsible for the vicious circle these conditions create. Our uncritical acceptance of inferior, useless, or unnecessary goods has made the creation of an artificial, and consequently a fluctuating, market all too easy. Besides producing a distortion of values within the factory, this kind of market produces similar distortions without. The main effort of those who manufacture is to fill the demand, real or induced, of those people who have the most money with which to buy. From the manufacturer's point of view, a product that is useless, or even harmful, is more profitable to produce if people with purchasing power can be induced to buy it, than one for which there is a genuine need among the less fortunate. Any exploration of means to supply an entire population with the things it really needs has not often been the concern of those who produce. Here again human values are sacrificed. If an artificial market were not so easily created, such exploration might well become expedient.

Advertising propaganda may be used for other things besides the creation of a market for tangible products. It may be used for selling ideas and for influencing attitudes and behavior. Machines have made the widespread dissemination of news and information possible. It becomes increasingly difficult to distinguish between *bona-fide* news and news that has been selected or slanted in some way. The same play on the emotions which is used to such good effect in advertising can be used, and is being used, by the press in its relaying of news.

The ease and perfection of communication which the use of the machine affords, therefore, has its inherent dangers as well as its immense potentialities for good. The unconsidered enthusiasm with which we have welcomed these agents of communication has laid us wide open to their dangers. Intelligent criticism of the printed and spoken word as it comes to us through the press, the movie, and the radio is becoming increasingly necessary if we are to keep even a semblance of independent thought and action.

The world of the machine, then, can not be uncritically accepted. If we are to keep the enormous benefits of machinery, and at the same time keep first things first—things such as human personality, the free functioning of human capabilities, a healthy social life—we must be able somehow to separate the wheat from the chaff.

There has been much publicity given lately to the Amish sect of Pennsylvania Germans who have refused to send their children to a central county school. The main reason they gave for this stand was that they did not wish their children to be exposed to the machines and the machine-made products, the radios, the movies, etc., that were to be found at the central school. These they have deliberately and consistently kept out of their own communities. The Amish folk prefer to have their children grow up in a well-assimilated environment, one that is understandable to them and that they can control. One can not help admiring them for taking so positive a stand and winning their point. But to renounce the machine is not a realistic way out. For the majority of us it would be an impossible and unworthy retreat. What can we do, as parents, to meet the situation?

II

Attitudes toward the World of the Machine

WHAT BASIC ATTITUDES DO WE WISH TO DEVELOP TOWARD the world of the machine?

The marks of a good manipulator. Although we can use machines without knowing in detail how they work, we must at least know enough to keep them in good running order. For safety and efficiency, something more is needed. The person who uses a tool should have a very clear idea of *what* it does, even if his ideas about *how* it is done are hazy. The child who uses a saw should know how sharp and ruthless its teeth are; the adolescent who drives an automobile should be able to imagine the immense damage and human misery a carelessly handled mechanism of such size and mobility can cause. No one who does not have a very real sense of its potentialities, dangerous as well as useful, should have control of any machine.

Tools are made to be manipulated. Is the attitude of a good manipulator, then, all we need to foster? No, we have seen how easily, in modern life, the tables can be turned and the machines make the men jump. To put machines in their place—as extensions and supplements of human beings—is as important as putting man in his place, in nature. Can something like the participator's attitude to nature be translated into the machine world?

Assimilating the machine world. Understanding, ordering, and cherishing may sound sentimental applied to an "iron chaos." But the machine age is chaos only if we fail to assimilate it.

Children approach machinery with emotional zest. It is, as much as other parts of their world, a stimulus for play and art. This will not be news to any one familiar with their spontaneous painting and writing. Four-year-olds go into rhapsodies over the great biting steam-shovel; older children, over the electric eye that finds the flaw in a tin can passing by on a factory conveyer-belt. It is important to keep this interest and sensitivity alive. All we have said about the artist's attitude toward nature applies as well here.

After all, exploring the man-made contraptions by which we live is not so different from exploring nature. A house, for example, whether it has two stories or fifteen, is a functioning thing. By means of it man sets up the living conditions he needs, providing water, protection from wind and rain, power for light, heat, and cooking. Children—and grown-ups, too, to judge by the inevitable group of onlookers at any building job—are fascinated to watch a house grow from groundwork to skeleton to functioning reality. But even before this fascination grips them, young children are interested in ex-

Children approach machinery with emotional zest. It is, as much as other parts of their world, a stimulus for play and art.

ploring their own house. This is an interest that can grow and lead out in many ways. At four or five, children might explore the water system—where the water comes in, how it gets to the heater, where the pipes are that take it to the various faucets. At eight or nine the community water system can be encompassed, from reservoir to homes. At thirteen or fourteen, processes may become linked to the social problems bound up with them, leading into city or rural planning, how rates are determined, and such questions. And so with many paths that start at home.

First-hand investigation is important, and parents can do much to encourage it. And the mechanical world, as well as nature, lends itself to classification. There are machines for extending man's sensory equipment—telescopes, thermometers, seismographs. There are machines for converting one form of energy to another—dynamos, water-turbines, motors; for speeding or slowing the application of force; and so on. To think of machines in this way orders old experiences, gives them added meaning, and opens the way for new ones.

Actually handling machines both deepens and tests the attitudes being developed in other ways. Here the human problem, the problem of putting machines in their place, comes up most plainly.

When does one use a tool? A tool is used to ensure a performance which, unaided, (1) could not be done at all, (2) could not be done satisfactorily, (3) could not be done with a reasonable expenditure of time and energy. The slaves employed by Egyptian masters to erect the pyramids could not have done their task at all without the assistance of such mechanical devices as the wheel, the lever, and the pulley. Yet even with these tools, the expenditure of time and energy necessary for the building of the pyramids staggers us to-day. Our own skyscrapers could never have been built if we depended on the same amount of human labor, the same expenditure of time and energy. Human beings are too valuable to be used up in this way. It is mainly due to our machines that we are in a position to recognize and appreciate that fact, and at the same time to get jobs as colossal as pyramid-building done.

The use of machinery is a matter of judgment. It is evident, then, that as far as 2 and 3 are concerned, the use of a tool is a relative matter. What constitutes a satisfactory performance or a reasonable expenditure of time and energy varies greatly with existing conditions. It also varies with the special requirements of the person who proposes to use the tool. It becomes, therefore, a matter of judgment. A manipulator must be able to ask himself these questions: Is this use of machinery saving time and energy where they need to be saved? Are other desirable satisfactions, which a more laborious handling might give, being thoughtlessly discarded by such use?

Evaluating the machine in terms of our homes. We have repeated opportunities to debate these questions in our homes, for our homes have become increasingly dependent on machines. Much of our food is grown many miles away and is transported by machinery; much of it is preserved or processed for use in factories; a lot of it is partially or entirely prepared for the table before it is bought. Our clothing is almost entirely made by large-scale production methods, and it is for the most part kept clean and repaired in the same way. Most of our equipment (furniture, utensils, decorations, etc.) is also ready-made. What this amounts to is that any one family group does very little in the way of providing directly for its own needs. We have our much-lauded leisure, but it has proved to be a mixed blessing.

In the family of a few generations ago, everyday living had a different pattern. The kitchen was a busier place. There was less ready money, and people consequently relied more upon their own ingenuity and initiative to make a home valuable. More activity centered there. There were consequently more things for every member of the family to do. This activity had an importance that was little realized until the need for it began to disappear. People get on better together when they are engaged in common activities. This is not true only of families. When it is necessary to work together as well as to be together, all groups run more smoothly. A sustaining, vigorous round of activity is a healthy condition for any social group. If we consider families important, then, it may be wise to think twice before relegating so much of their normal activity to machinery, especially machinery that functions outside the home.

Purposeful activity not only helps to keep group living running smoothly, however; the homes where a variety of activity went on were good educational centers, too. It is not only because our ideas about education have changed that school programs give so much more emphasis than they formerly did to constructive activity, to doing as well as thinking. When activity necessarily went on at home, children did not need to rely so heavily on the schools for what they learned. Education meant "book" learning, but in the handling of tools, the cooking of meals, the making of clothes, much important education went on at home. Now school programs have to provide for this kind of learning, too.

Much of the activity that was necessary in homes before labor-saving devices were in general use was, of course, drudgery. There is a legitimate distinction here. Labor that is repetitious and that produces little in the way of a tangible product can be relegated to machinery, to be dispensed with as quickly and efficiently as possible. Cleaning jobs are in this class. The more efficient machinery one can afford for these purposes, the better. But there are many home jobs that make demands on ingenuity and give valuable satisfaction in the doing. These are the ones that deserve consideration before they are handed over to the machine. The manufactured furniture we buy may be more skilfully turned, yet the end-table made at a home work-bench may be more satisfactory for the thrill of accomplishment and pride that use of it gives.

Many home jobs are of this kind, giving scope for initiative, experiment, talent, and some artistic ability. These are the jobs through which one learns. Even though schools

The kitchen is another place where opportunities for worth-while jobs are many and varied. Cooking presents golden opportunities for children over seven.

are developing more rounded programs, it seems foolish for parents to overlook these opportunities that come so easily to hand, fit so naturally into our living together.

Home decoration is such an opportunity. Pride in one's surroundings is considerably enhanced by having a direct share, no matter how small, in their creation. A family work-bench, where some of the things we use are constructed, can give children this sense. Wooden book-ends, paper-weights, and the like can be successfully made by the five-year-old. As he grows more proficient in the use of tools, he can help out on bigger jobs—the making of a table or a needed set of shelves.

If space does not permit the use of carpenter's tools, there are other handicrafts that can contribute to family furnishings. Metal and leather work can supply such things as ash trays and covers for books; a small loom can turn out luncheon sets and table throws; linoleum blocks can decorate kitchen and bathroom curtains or make the family greeting cards.

These are only a few of the multiple possibilities. The main thing is to give each member of the family a chance to contribute something constructive to family needs. It is well to learn early in life that one's own time, thought, and labor transformed into a tangible product give such a product a value of a special kind not to be bought with money.

The kitchen is another place where opportunities for worth-while jobs are many and varied. Cooking presents golden opportunities for children over seven. Now that baking has been made practically fool-proof by modern equipment, the whole process of cooky-making or of baking a simple layer cake can be undertaken by the seven-year-old. And how much better such a cake tastes, even though it is not a professional job, than the one from the corner bakery! If he is reading on his own, it is a good idea to write or print out the recipe to be used by a young cook in clear, understandable language. Even though some supervision may be necessary, having clear instructions to follow gives the job an independent air that is very gratifying.

When a child becomes more used to the procedures of cooking, he can take over a meal on his own. Delegating Sunday night supper to the children once in a while is a good way of giving them a chance to take the initiative. There are many simple one-dish meals that can be handled entirely by an eight-year-old, provided some adult forethought is given to the subject.

All this does not mean that we ought, *ipso facto*, to return to an earlier, handicraft stage of living in our homes. Not at all. But it does mean that it is wise to keep a sense of perspective, to evaluate our uses of machinery by taking into account other things besides the greater efficiency, the time-and-energy-saving usefulness, of the machine. We are in a much more advantageous position than were the parents of another day in this respect, for we can pick and choose. The drudgery can be efficiently despatched. Out of the interesting jobs we can build a program of purposeful activity, of doing, that will not only prove interesting but may well help to make our families more stable affairs. This ability to put machines in their place is the best contribution home life can make toward a more humane use of machinery in our national life.

III

A Child's Use of Machinery and Its Products

WHEN SHOULD CHILDREN USE MACHINERY? THE TEST OF a manipulator applies to children and adults equally. No one, whatever his age, should control a mechanism whose effects he is incapable of estimating. As for judging the relative values in the use of machinery, not until they are of age do young people take full responsibility. But certainly much sooner they should be aware that judgments are being made, should know the reasons for and gradually take more and more part in family decisions. And they begin to take real, though not complete, responsibility when we give them an allowance.

From children under six or seven we can not expect much in the way of a conscious attitude. But through the playthings we choose for them we set up habits that will powerfully affect their later decisions. In making choices for them we must think, then, of the larger issues and of children's own special needs.

The well-equipped workshop of a small private school contained, among other things, a power-saw. All the children who had shop work, beginning with a group of six-year-olds, used this power-saw. But neither of the reasons for using machinery is likely to weigh with the average six-year-old. His critical appreciation of the table or toy auto he is making in the shop has not matured enough so that the greater accuracy of a machine-cut edge makes any difference to him. The saving of time and energy makes no difference to him either. In fact, the process itself is fully as important at six as is any resulting product. Time and energy spent in that process have special satisfactions of their own at that age. It is quite otherwise when one is eleven or twelve and used enough to work in the shop to be mainly interested in turning out a well-finished, workmanlike job. Then the power-saw has distinct advantages.

One can make a broad but useful generalization from this example of the power-saw. If a process is new and unfamiliar, there is an advantage for a child in doing it for itself. Any speeding-up or short-cutting should then be avoided. We must remember, too, that during the early period of body growth, from babyhood to adolescence, a child's own body is his most effective tool. What he can accomplish with his own hands and arms and legs should, to a large extent, be accomplished that way. He needs variety in his activity to give him a physical outlet as well as to help him acquire a number of different skills. For this reason, too, the simpler, more laborious way of doing things is often the better way for him.

A child's possessions. From the thrilling moment when a baby discovers that he can hold on to and manipulate a separate object he becomes a user of machine-made goods.

From then on, such goods are one of the pervading factors in his life. The three-year-old looks forward to the surprise in Daddy's pocket every evening; the six-year-old becomes a connoisseur of toy automobiles; the eight-year-old saves his allowance to buy the latest intriguing gadget displayed in the window of a corner store. By the time a child is ten or twelve years old he is a full-fledged and often omnivorous consumer, as easily manipulated by skilful advertising as are his elders.*

Precautions against an uncritical exposure to advertising begin, then, with a child's possessions and their acquisition. By encouraging certain habits, we can do a lot to fortify children against unthinking acceptance of the printed word. In the first place, *use* is the fundamental reason for possession, and this fact deserves emphasis. Possessions do give one a sense of importance and of being placed; they do serve to outline a personality, to etch its uniqueness in deeper lines. But possessions that have a use in themselves can do this just as well as, in fact better than, those which are merely hoarded.

The best way to emphasize usefulness in a child's possessions is to see that the things he owns are appropriate for his use. This means, first of all, that they should be appropriate in themselves, well adapted to the use for which they are intended. Wheel-toys should be durable, well designed, and easily manipulated. Tools and instruments, though of a smaller size, should be just as durable

* The fact that a good-sized book entitled *Reaching Juvenile Markets* has been published by a well-known house is significant in this connection.

What he can accomplish with his own hands and arms and legs should, to a large extent, be accomplished that way.

and designed to do their job just as well as similar ones intended for adult use. Materials for experimenting (specific materials such as chemical sets, photographer's outfits, and the like, as well as raw materials such as blocks, paints, etc.) should be supplied in sufficient quantities to make their use worth while.

In brief, the fact that something is designed for a child's use, and technically classed as a toy, is no excuse for shoddiness or inadequacy. The continued use of poorly made things that break readily, or of things which never seem to do what one expects of them, has its inevitable results. The child whose toy shelf is strewn with broken or discarded things, whose prized possessions are continually having to be replaced, becomes careless and often destructive. His possessions form no continuity through which he may express himself. He becomes, as a consequence, ready prey for those who later rely on him continually to buy the newest thing.

If they are to be genuinely useful, possessions should not only be appropriate in themselves but appropriate for use by the person to whom they belong. Boxing-gloves may be a very worth-while gift to the nine-year-old but they can have no real place among the possessions of a four-year-old. Boys are quite different creatures at four and at nine. Interests and abilities change rapidly with growth. We have to take these changes into account. Reliable guides to the average interests of most ages are now available to parents. By observing what use is made of a new possession one can learn a lot. Does it carry on a previous interest in a constructive way? Does its use help a child to carry on some project of his own? What can he *do* with it?

In the main, possessions should serve the ends of their owners, not for a passing moment but in some more permanent way. They should offer opportunities for initiative as well as for imitation; scope for creative and inventive ability as well as for group team work. Many of the toys that flood our markets are not particularly helpful in this respect. They are "end-product" toys. One can only do one thing with them; they are designed for only one purpose. These are the kinds of toys that are used only for a short time and then discarded for something else. They have little lasting value. There is a quick turnover when they dominate the toy shelves.

Children who are in the habit of using this kind of toy are much more susceptible to the pressures of advertising. They become accustomed to looking for a new thrill, a different quirk, in their toys. They come to depend on what the toy can do, not on what they can do with the toy. As they grow older they are much more likely to use other products of the machine in the same way. They expect to be entertained instead of finding something which they can use to entertain themselves.

Sometimes, it is true, interests and abilities do not seem to jibe. The shiny new bicycle or the brand-new baseball bat of a ten-year-old brother or neighbor whose deeds are already haloed may seem very desirable to a five-year-old. However, neither one fills a useful need at this age, but only an imitative one. The best way to get around this difficulty is to provide many opportunities for the kind of activity that is appropriate at five; then, whenever possible, to foster such mutual understanding and appreciation between children of different ages as will give the younger child a sense of the importance of his kind of activity as well as admiration for his elders' pursuits.

With so many enticing displays in the stores, many of us find ourselves becoming involved in miscellaneous purchases before we know it. One mother said to me, "I can't take Billy shopping with me any more, he makes such a nuisance of himself!" She had been in the habit of buying something from the five-and-ten every so often when she and Billy did the morning's shopping. These odds and ends had become very important to Billy, and if she did not stop to collect something or other, he made a fuss. None of these things lasted very long. Many of them Billy didn't really want after he got them home. The idea of getting something new was paramount. Of course, that's what the displays are for, and unless we are careful, we are all of us, children and adults alike, easily imposed upon.

One has to be adamant, sometimes, in self-defense. A good way, if such purchases are sometimes made, is to be quite definite about limiting them. The five-and-ten can be visited once every two weeks as a regular treat instead of now and then at shorter and shorter intervals. If Billy had known beforehand that this was not the day to go to the five-and-ten, there would have been no chance for argument.

Another help is to make children themselves realize the uselessness of much of the display. We can do this by suggesting needs beforehand. There are many small objects that fit well into the five-year-old's block play, for instance. A little conversation before one goes out can help to direct purchases a bit. If one goes to the store with a definite idea that a small red auto would be very nice to use, or that a small string of freight cars would be fun to have now that one is interested in building railroad tracks and pretending to carry all sorts of things to the city, there will not be nearly so much temptation to pick things indiscriminately.

If we wish to stress the usefulness of possessions, not only must they be appropriate; they must be owned in reasonable quantity. Here is another reason for not visiting the five-and-ten too often. The child who has more things than he can reasonably use is likely to become more interested in acquisition than in use, like Billy. Superfluous possessions are bound to collect, fond relatives being what they are. One can get around this dilemma by having a storage closet where reserves are kept. The available supply can then be reduced to a usable minimum and one can provide variety by changing it from time to time as shifts in interest occur.

Billy, at five, was beginning to make his own purchases. Even at this age, grown-ups do not have complete control of the purse-strings; children's own wishes come to the fore. Older children are usually given an allowance. What then? How much should we have to say about the things a child buys for himself with his own money?

A child's allowance. There are several ways of arranging a child's allowance. In some families remuneration is given for specific tasks, and this money a child is free to spend as he sees fit. This arrangement rather puts the cart before the horse. Gilbert sees something in a store window that particularly intrigues him. Before he sees it, nothing is further from his mind than mowing the lawn. But now he hurries home in a dither to be useful. True, this gives him the idea that money must be earned to be spent, and he must want the coveted article very much to give some time to earning it. However, it does overemphasize the object in the store window. Isolated spending of this kind does not help to keep the alluring displays in any kind of perspective. Gilbert should be mowing the lawn because the lawn needs mowing, not because he wants something from a store. Sporadic wealth of this kind does not help children to evaluate and plan their expenditures.

A certain amount of money is often given a child regularly. If this has no strings attached to it, if the spending of it depends only on his own caprice, with no pressure of necessity and no recognition of his own part in the family expenses, we are quite likely to have trouble. If money is spent in this kind of vacuum, it is much more apt to be spent impulsively, and a lot more trash is collected.

One can also go to the other extreme. The two youngsters of one family were given the liberal allowance of fifty cents a week. Ten cents of this was designated for the collection plate in Sunday school; ten cents was to be put in the bank; with the remainder they were expected to buy a buttonhole flower for their mother every Friday and something for themselves.

An allowance can be managed so that it gives a child the chance to make real decisions and to weigh the chances of getting something he really wants against a few necessities. The necessities do not need to be arbitrarily imposed, however. Buying school supplies out of his allowance is a good idea. Putting aside, for a child to draw on, an amount large enough for all his expenses is also a possibility. However, this usually presents the younger child with too complicated a problem, one which requires too much adult supervision. It makes a more satisfactory arrangement for the adolescent; by this time children are more interested in the expenditures that have to be made for clothes and other personal items.

Even the seven-year-old can understand that the ten cents he is allowed every week is part of the family budget and is only one of the expenses paid out for him. One seven-year-old wanted very much to have a special electric engine for his trains. He was told that this was impossible at the moment. After some argument, his father showed him the accounts for the past month, including what had been spent for him. He explained that there was only so much money for all the things the family needed, and that it would not cover the cost of an electric engine. It was Arthur's own suggestion that he save his allowance and buy the engine with that when he had enough.

Once the amount of a child's allowance has been set, there should be no additions to solve the problems of poor management. If there is no money with which to buy a needed notebook, the inconvenience of not having it until funds are due again will encourage more careful management the next time. Just what expenditures any allowance is expected to cover, and the fact that no other money will be available for those expenditures, should be made very clear at the outset. If these terms are kept consistently, a child's control of his own allowance will not raise many questions of dubious purchases. He will learn to be critical of his purchases and to apportion his money thoughtfully among them.

IV

A Child's Use of the Propaganda Products of Machinery: Radio, Press, and Motion-Picture

THERE ARE TWO PRODUCTS OF THE MACHINE THAT COME into almost every home and exert tremendous influence upon all the family. These are the radio and the newspaper. Because their influence is so great, and because they are bound to be a real part of almost any family atmosphere, they deserve some detailed discussion here.

Use of the radio. The radio is a machine. However, most of us use it on the consumer end, as we do books or other sources of information and entertainment. It is what the radio produces that is important. Here, at the turn of a dial, a gesture that the merest toddler can manage, the whole outside world suddenly blares into our living-rooms: cheap entertainment, performances by the world's greatest artists, the tense drama of political events, stray bits of information and consecutive attempts to inform, passing styles in behavior, language, and thought.

There are two problems that a promiscuous use of the radio inevitably presents in a family with children. In the first place, such a use raises all sorts of questions prematurely. Dramatic sketches and the like bring unfamiliar mores and social problems to the attention of children long before they have any basis for judging or understanding them. Moreover, these unfamiliarities are often presented in ways that give them unfortunate and undesirable connotations. Then there is the matter of advertising. The ether waves are filled to-day with skilled and ingenious advertising, a good deal of which is especially designed to reach young listeners. Radio advertising is particularly successful with children, for they are used to attending the spoken word. The appeal of written words does not have the same dramatic immediacy for them.

There has been much discussion of children's radio programs. But a wise choice of these would not solve our problem in itself. It is the accessibility of miscellaneous and unpredictable items that is the chief difficulty. It is so easy to turn the dial, and almost anything is likely to come out. We grown-ups ourselves so often have bad radio habits. We turn on a radio without any idea of what we want to hear, merely to have an agreeable noise somewhere in the background. We leave it to go on from one kind of entertainment to another without any real attention. Even when the program is something we intended to enjoy, we carry on desultory conversation, wander about the house, and listen only spasmodically. No wonder that children come to treat the radio casually, too.

The first step toward control of this powerful medium, then, is a vigorous stock-taking of our own habits. Do we really listen to the music that comes out of the loudspeaker, according unseen performers the same courtesy of attention that prevails in the concert hall? Do the quips and pranks of the entertainers really fill a need for release, for salutary laughter? Or do we merely listen because every one else listens and because a given time on a given night means tuning to a given spot on the dial? Are we tied to a radio, giving it the time that might otherwise be spent in some activity of our own instead of in passive listening to the activities of others? An honest and thoughtful answering of these questions should show how much we control the radio and how much the radio has come to control us.

If it is controlled, the radio can fill a real and valuable place in family life. One family has worked out a method of radio-listening which gets the most out of it for them without unduly sacrificing other things. On Sundays, the week's radio programs are looked over by all the family, and each one makes a choice of what he would like to hear. The children are allowed three different programs each, during the week. These must fall somewhere within the hours immediately preceding or following dinner, so that they do not interfere with either outdoor play or ordinary routine. When the choices are made, there is usually some discussion about them, and finally a list is made of days and times, to be posted near the radio. This list constitutes the radio's use during that week. It is not turned on otherwise, unless something out of the ordinary turns up. The children never turn it on except when their choice of a program occurs. If Mary has chosen a musical program that takes place on Wednesday at 6:30, it is her

If it is controlled, the radio can fill a real and valuable place in family life.

prerogative to operate the radio at that time. The other children may listen or not, as they please; but if they do not listen, their activities must be carried on elsewhere, so as not to interfere with Mary's enjoyment of the material she wanted to hear.

This may seem an arbitrary arrangement to the outsider, but it has never seemed so to the family concerned. Their radio has always been used that way. It has contributed not a little to the enlarging of boundaries and interests in different ways. For a time, Mary listened regularly to a short violin recital that she enjoyed for the inspiration it gave to her own violin-playing. Jim relied on talks from the local museum to help him in his unraveling of the heavens. And so it went. Each week the radio brought something of interest that was attentively listened to and often used.

Undesirable choices were also made, of course. Once nine-year-old Jim was much taken by the reports of his schoolmates on a particularly bloodthirsty tale about cattle-rustlers. The cattle-rustlers held forth intermittently for a while. Not for long, however. Jim's father enjoyed a good "western" himself. He took this occasion to introduce his son to some of his own favorites and Jim soon became impatient with the inferior radio script. In fact, a new interest sprang up that completely superseded radio-listening for a while, so far as Jim was concerned. The attic was ransacked for old magazines with pictures of the West. The library was besieged for information about ranch life and the hazards of cattle-raising. Enthusiasm was aroused for a western auto trip. Thus, what began as an interest in shouting and shooting became the basis for a worth-while exploration of a different kind of life in an unknown part of the country.

Such a controlled use of the radio makes it much easier to deal with the problems it creates. Undesirable material and excessive advertising appeal can be kept to a minimum. As children grow older we can help them to be critical of the advertising they hear. They can be made conscious of the innumerable devices used to promote sales; of the attempts to push a product legitimately useful in one way into wider, less rational, use; of the exaggerated claims resorted to in order to meet competition. Even a child can be alert to these advertising habits, and much advertising is so crude that even a child's judgment is insulted thereby. Surely even the eight-year-old can not take seriously the claims that a certain breakfast food will, by itself, make him strong, keep him well, help him to succeed both on the baseball diamond and at school, and make him popular with other children!

Little children have no real occasion to use a radio at all. There is little that it offers which holds the attention of a child until he is seven or eight years old. Radio music is not often simple enough for younger ears. Moreover, little children enjoy repetition in their music. Phonograph records that one can hear again and again are much better suited to their tastes. It is a sorry world, indeed, where one's story has to be told by a disembodied presence out of the air. Three-quarters of the joy of being told a story, when one is three or even four, is sitting close to the person who tells it, looking at the pictures together, guessing what is coming next.

To the small child, therefore, the radio can remain an adult prerogative. We insist that the three-year-old leave the cocks of a gas stove alone, as a protection to him. The switch of the radio is in the same class; it operates something that is of no use to him and that is, like the gas stove, beyond his control. If he is in the habit of turning it on and off at will before the sounds that come out have much meaning to him, we will have much more of a problem to cope with when we wish him to discriminate. If children begin to use a radio only when it can be of some genuine use to them, desirable habits are much more easily formed. Many of us are distressed by the material offered in children's programs, but not so many of us realize that the difficulties begin when the two-year-old trots across the room and switches on the radio, thrilled beforehand by the blare of noise that he knows will come out.

We can emphasize the radio's use for older children by tying some of its programs into family interests. One municipal station recently gave a series of programs describing the activities of the city departments. Here was a golden opportunity to make the radio serve a worthwhile purpose. Family trips could well have supplemented the material of the broadcasts. Musical programs can be supplemented by reading and by use of phonograph records. Many radio programs make suggestions for further exploration of their subject matter. By following up a few of these as a family undertaking, we can make passive listening lead to activity of some kind. Good entertainment can be the occasion for a family get-together. Programs that are listened to in this way make a contribution to comradely enjoyment that is worth while, too. If children become familiar with the radio by using it, they will learn to keep it in its place and not themselves be used.

Interpreting the press. The written word, too, invades our homes, but not so insistently nor so unpredictably as the radio. We know beforehand what to expect in the way of sensationalism and distorted news-handling from individual papers and magazines. By deliberate choice, the less desirable ones can be excluded altogether. However, even the most dignified journalism descends at times to what it considers the level of its public. The good and the bad are often sadly mixed. Moreover, sensationalism is not the only problem. The most sedate journalism, if it deals with unfamiliar, uncomprehended facts, can be just as confusing and misleading as a sensational handling would be.

Cartoons, news photographs, and now the picture magazines convey their impressions to children even before they can read. There seems to be a strange, yet general, misconception about pictures. Due perhaps to the tradition of the picture book, any printed picture is considered fit material for children. Such sophisticated and confusing material as is contained in the weekly picture magazines is handed on to small children on no better basis than that "children like to look at pictures." The same can be said of cartoons. The subjects of most of these, their humor and their story content, are beyond any genuine understanding or appreciation by children. If we attempt to explain, we almost always get into deep water of some kind. The only childlike thing about them is their oversimplification, their black-and-white handling of situations.

To any one who is concerned about a child's awareness of human relationships, his sensitivity to human values, these news photographs are often ghastly affairs. The five-year-old youngster may not grasp at all the meaning of the pictured court-room scene or the confusion of the picket-line forced to defend itself. But the tense and anxious expressions of the pictured faces, the dramatic quality of conflict caught by the camera, does convey something to him. Unexplained and often unexplainable, it nevertheless leaves its impression.

It is not so much that we seek to shield children from either the sordidness or the complexities of living, but that too early exposure to these things produces what might be called a callousness of uncomprehension. To become familiar with crime, with misguided and desperate human behavior, even with the vagaries that the cartoonists make amusing, long before one can have any comprehension of their import, not only is grossly misleading; it also blunts sensibilities.

It blunts one's sense of responsibility, too. We are legitimately separate from the dramatic end-results portrayed in the pictures. Responsibility for the multiple causes which precipitated them, however, we all must share. If children become familiar with these things through their end-results, this social responsibility will be so much the harder for them to develop. The mature person has a perspective and a frame of reference into which he can fit these things. He can infer from his own experience many of the causes that lie back of them. Children have no such perspective. We cease to be curious about the things that are familiar. If children come to accept the strike, the suicide, the theft, as among the things that are, before they can put these things into an appropriate social setting, they may never be curious enough about the whys and wherefores that bring them about. It is part of our job to protect them from too early familiarity and to keep curiosity alive.

We can not protect children entirely from these crass glimpses into adult living, of course. The camera has made them too easily available for that. But we can try to minimize them. So far as small children are concerned, the magazines with pictures belong among the things that are understood to be adult possessions and are respected as such.

Even before they can read news for themselves, children often find themselves in the midst of situations that are incomprehensible to them. The buzz of publicity that attends a political campaign, a social scandal, a serious industrial strike, or an international crisis surrounds them with ill-assorted scraps that they pick up and use in self-defense, wishing to be part of the commotion, too. We can not disregard this entirely. If we wish to help them find their way in this maze, we must think through some method of adequate interpretation.

It may give us pause to know what weight such interpretations have. During the first World War my father explained the aggression of Germany thus: "Suppose you had a shiny new bicycle, but were told you couldn't use it, that it must be kept in the back yard. That wouldn't be very easy to do, would it? Some day you would probably take it out on the street anyway. Well, that's what happened in Germany. She had an army of which she was very proud, just as you would be proud of the new bicycle. She wasn't supposed to use it, but one day the temptation was too great, and she did."

This analogy was a very telling one, since new bicycles were at the moment much in my mind. To this day, the armies of preparedness seem like so many shiny bicycles, waiting to be wheeled out.

Early interpretations are very apt to leave lasting impressions of this kind. That is why we have to be careful in thinking them through. The analogy of the bicycle and the German army was all right so far as it went, but it did not go far enough. That the preparedness of the army was only a contributing factor in a complicated situation was also important to understand.

The interpretations we give to events will, of course, be colored by our own reactions to the things that are taking place. We should, however, be careful in two ways: we should try to steer clear of labels, and we should try to make our interpretations go deeper than an emotional response. Labels and emotions are too easy to trade on. Even the seven-year-old can be helped to a critical attitude. By explaining what we can in terms of causes, and by admitting that there are things about which we do not know enough to pass judgment, we can do a lot in this respect.

Only by being constantly critical of the instruments through which we get our news can we hope to be able to evaluate it. Children can be helped to develop a salutarily critical attitude toward newspapers and magazines as they approach adolescence and begin to use them independently. We can make them conscious of the discrepancies and biases of reported news in a number of ways.

Every newspaper reader should acquire the habit of comparing the actual texts of important news stories with the head-lines that top them. Such a habit guards against a certain amount of bias. It is always better to read at least two newspapers or magazines whose editorial policies differ, to get different slants on the same story. The differences may not strike any profound issue, but the fact that they occur is the important thing of which to be aware. Children can acquire these habits as soon as they do any appreciable reading on their own.

Experiments in reporting events one's self are also a help in understanding the limitations of the newspapers. The fact that two different people will remember the same happening differently, will even see it differently, is one that is very easy to demonstrate and one that merits repeated demonstration.

Family discussions can also help in evaluating one's own use of newspaper material. Is the opinion contributed by fourteen-year-old John a considered one, formed by reading several accounts; or it is a snap judgment gleaned from a cursory reading of head-lines? It is well to learn early how to be critical of one's own mass of information, to be alert to one's own biases, and to be aware that the basis for a genuine opinion of any kind must be the result of considered reading from more than one source. All these things can be brought out by discussion.

Some one has suggested that children be taught from the very beginning never to make a statement of fact without also giving its authority. For instance, instead of saying "The Green Mountains are in Vermont," one should say, "The geography book says that the Green Mountains are in Vermont." All statements that have no confirmation from one's own senses and experience should have their authority tacked on. This may be extreme, but it has a point. Especially in matters of opinion and in current situations this habit can be very useful. We can preface our own explanations in this way and expect children to do the same when they are telling about something that they have read. Instead of saying "Two policemen were hurt in a fight with pickets," one can say, "The *Times* article says that two policemen were hurt in a fight with pickets." This is also a useful device in dealing with advertising.

Use of the motion-picture. The motion-picture, though not penetrating our homes directly, influences us quite as much as do the radio and the press. It has a tremendous effect on the customs and thought of a community. It is a convenient medium of relaxation and escape. Its carefully controlled censorship acts to preserve our morals, both political and social, as well as our religious faith. Here is a weapon even more powerful than the press, for its entertainment value and its direct, emotional appeal make it much more effective on large groups of people. As a vital educational medium, it is more effective than our schools. Such a powerful product of the machine deserves to be dealt with warily, to say the least.

The movies open up a whole complex world to children. In this respect their influence is much like that of the news photographs and the cartoons. They introduce elements which are beyond a child's comprehension and familiarize him with situations and relationships long before he can rightly estimate or criticize them. They penetrate his life even more realistically than do the picture magazines, for their dramatic sequence is easily carried over into his play. Gangsters, army pilots, G-men, and all the rest step from the screen to act their rôles in neighborhood lots and city streets.

Movies, even those designed for children, do not legitimately enter a child's life until he is at least seven or eight. The nervous strain of following the pictures, the sitting still, the optical adjustments necessary over a prolonged period, are all factors that must be considered where younger children are concerned. Moreover, most of the movies designed for children are too involved to have much meaning for this young audience. There are positive reasons, too, why movie-going should be a deferred pleasure for the four- or five-year-old. There are so many other things to do! So many other ways of being amused or of having a good time! Sitting still in darkness, watching the activities of others, may have some sense at a later period, but when one considers how active and how fond of space and light a healthy five-year-old youngster is, such a performance seems merely ridiculous. Dramatics, at five, are something in which to take part, not something to watch. If we consider a young child's own welfare, then, and his own best interests, the problems of movie-going do not even begin for him.

The age at which movies do begin to be a worth-while form of entertainment depends somewhat on the individual child. When one considers how much of the waking day is necessarily spent in school during the week, it seems almost criminal to spend precious afternoon hours sitting indoors. There are many other things that can be done on Saturdays and Sundays. If we have provided the means for varied and constructive activity, there will be little time for movie-going. An occasional family party on Saturday afternoon to take in a movie that has some meaning for all concerned should be all that any child between the ages of seven and ten either needs or wants.

Any one who has watched children, most of them from ten to fifteen years of age, trooping into a moving-picture theater on a bright, sunny Saturday morning can not fail to realize that the movie habit is of early growth. There are, of course, many reasons why the movies are patronized so liberally at this age. Lack of space at home and inadequate outdoor facilities both play an important part. But it is not only the city theaters that have their juvenile movie fans. Children who have large yards in which to play and work and ample indoor space about which to strew their belongings, spend time at the movies.

One can not help wondering whether this early and

overdeveloped taste for the vicarious is not simply a further search for the sensational thrill that is supplied first by highly mechanized toys, toys that emphasize speed and noise and the simple attainment of highly dramatic effects —the press-the-trigger and push-the-button kind of toy. But this is not the whole answer. The young adolescent's devotion to the movies goes deeper than this.

During the pre-adolescent and early adolescent years, children are increasingly curious about adult behavior and about the personal relationships that characterize the adult world. They are often diffident about seeking such information directly, by asking questions. In fact, it is not an interpretation that they want at this time; it is the chance to see for themselves. The movies seem to give them that chance, for all kinds of people live on the screen, and all kinds of behavior are portrayed there.

If the movies are only one of a number of opportunities that children find for learning about the adult personal relationships that interest them, they can be worth while. But children must be given the means and encouragement to be critical of what they see. Uncritical acceptance of the movie world as reality or as an ideal to be emulated will not help them. The situations presented on the screen can often be the basis for a valuable exploration of opinions. Why did so-and-so act the way he did? Would we act the same way in a similar situation? Was the picture "real"? Or was it "just a story"? Then the screen drama can be profitably compared with similar material in other mediums and with its counterparts in literature. Finally, some knowledge of the technical side of movie-making—

the mechanics of putting a film together—and some realization of why screen dramas follow the patterns they do, give a child an objective attitude in relation to the glamour of filmdom that will stand him in good stead.

The best way of keeping the movies in their place is, of course, to see that children continue to have many opportunities for activity and exploration of their own; opportunities which, as children approach adolescence, take due account of growing social needs. If the early habits of doing for one's self and of thinking independently are well laid, even the new demands and interests of this age will not entirely overlay them. Children will be able to take what is worth while from the movies without becoming uncritical addicts.

Haphazard use of such powerful mediums as press, movies, and radio blunts our senses and imposes on us artificially the opinions of other minds. If we allow our freedom of thought to be weakened in this way, the very political institutions that guarantee our right to freedom are in danger. By developing a critical attitude, by teaching children to use rather than be used, we can subdue machines and their products to their legitimate place in a functioning human world. We can build and set children to building the dignified human existence to which machinery itself can so greatly contribute.

IV

The Outside World of People

I

Our Attitudes toward Other People: The Roots of Intolerance

IF WE VALUE THE FIRST PRINCIPLE OF DEMOCRACY—THAT individuals are valuable for themselves and for what they contribute to the commonweal—it is necessary to explore carefully our own attitudes toward other people. To review briefly our democratic history in this respect will give an interesting perspective.

Democracy flourished best under frontier conditions. The first settlements in New England were built on a communal plan. Even the settlements of Virginia, preserving more nearly the social distinctions of the Old World hierarchy, had to make democratic concessions to expediency. It was necessary, at first, to accept people for what they were individually and for what they could do. Later, as these seaboard colonies became established in trade, political and social barriers between peoples, similar to those of the settled European countries, grew up. But Americans had the good fortune to have frontiers for some time, and it was the frontiers that preserved the democratic tradition:

"The economy of the new West, essentially agricultural,

rested mainly upon a system of freehold farms. . . . For a long time there were in that vast region no merchant princes such as governed Philadelphia and Boston, no powerful landowning class comparable to the masters of the Hudson Valley manors. . . .

"For many decades, an overwhelming majority of the white men in the West were land-owning farmers. The unit of their society was the family on the isolated holding engaged in an unremitting battle with nature for its living. No benevolent government surrounded it with safeguards, no army of officials inspected its processes of life and labor. In a thousand emergencies it was thrown upon its own resources. . . .

"In its folkways and mores there was a rugged freedom —the freedom of the hardy men and women, taut of muscle and bronzed by sun and rain and wind, working with their hands in abundant materials. . . . Although travelers into the pioneer West disagreed on many points they were almost unanimous in enumerating the outstanding characteristics of the frontier people: independence in action, directness in manner, want of deference for ceremony, *willingness to make acquaintance with all sorts and conditions of mankind.*" *

On this western frontier people were again necessarily judged for themselves, and it was from this West that the support of Jeffersonian democracy came. Historically, then, the close connection between tolerance for other peo-

* Charles A. and Mary R. Beard, *The Rise of American Civilization* (New York, The Macmillan Company, 1927), Vol. I, pp. 534-35. Italics mine.

ple and the functioning of political democracy is clearly traceable.

The tolerance found in frontier communities was not, of course, the only factor in favor of their inherent democracy. But it played its distinctive part. It still plays a distinctive part in the democratic tradition. Now that the frontiers are largely gone and existing environmental conditions so often militate against it, such tolerance becomes very precious indeed to those who value democracy—the more so, as other political ideologies have shown only too clearly of late the close relationship between intolerance and democracy's destruction. Undermining forces invariably find in our intolerances, of whatever kind, rich ground to work. The reliance of democracy upon our attitudes toward other people is being, in our time, tragically proved.

Our society is made up in a peculiar way. We touched on its peculiarity when we considered the use of machinery. The family that supplies so few of its own needs is not only dependent on machinery; it is dependent on other people. How many persons do you suppose are involved in the growing, harvesting, and transporting of the dozen oranges you buy at the grocery store? I have no idea, but it must be a good many. If one wants the oranges, one is dependent on these people. So it goes with practically everything we use. We seldom think about these people, and when we do think about them, it is in abstract terms. They are "the working class" or "the transport workers' union" or "the fruit growers" or "the middlemen." Ordinarily, the only time we have occasion to refer to them is when difficulties of one kind or another arise; when, for one reason or another, the oranges do not arrive.

We are all dependent on other people, yet we do not feel our dependence. Our use of money obscures it for us. We are living in a society that is highly interdependent but poorly integrated. For an integrated society would be one in which dependence was felt. We need to put emotional content, human meanings, into the economy that makes us all dependent on each other. Only through more humane attitudes toward other people—people who are not in our immediate circle but who contribute materially to our welfare—can we achieve a more integrated democracy.

The nature of intolerance. There are many degrees of intolerance, from the subtly shaded differences in social customs and behavior to the rigid barriers of race and class. One can make this much of a generalization, however: Whenever a prejudicial statement is made of another person on the basis of his membership in a group (whether it be racial, religious, national, or class), intolerance is shown. It may, at the moment, be a latent intolerance, but this makes it no less dangerous.

Most of us are not aggressively intolerant. Under ordinary conditions we are merely aloof. We have an easygoing attitude of "live and let live," even though we may not be particularly interested in, or respectful of, the differences in people. They remain good fellows on the whole, though decidedly queer and often amusing.

But ordinary conditions do not always prevail.

When strains of one kind or another develop in a community, latent intolerances come to the surface very quickly. Then the people we thought queer actually begin to seem hateful. It is in times of economic depression that one hears a lot of talk about "aliens" and the bread they take out of other people's mouths. Other strains bring about much the same results. Whenever a community undergoes a wrench of any kind—aggressive labor organization, a shift in community status, an influx of population—these intolerances lose their aloof character. Moreover, as we have seen too well of late, they are always a potential danger as material for political manipulation.

It is not enough, therefore, to be critical of aggressive intolerance in others, or even to guard against it in our midst. The important thing is to make it impossible, as far as we can, by clearing up the latent feelings, the inarticulate prejudices, from which it springs. The conditions that stir up intolerance are often beyond our control, but we can do a lot toward seeing that there are no dregs to be stirred.

The sources of intolerance. Where do we get our prejudices? Where do the latent intolerances come from? There are three groups of people of whom we are likely to be intolerant: those who serve us; those who have a different background and different traditions; and those who have different social habits, who, in an established community, are the anti-social group. In each case, the reasons for intolerance are deep-seated. Their origins are to be found both in community history and in the psychology of individuals.

Broadly speaking, we are all servants of one another. But the use of money has obscured that fact. It makes possible a one-sided service that is rendered those who can pay. Domestic service is only a small part of this. There are servants without the home as well as within. We do not ordinarily think of the workers in the canning factory, the itinerant fruit and vegetable pickers, the men on the automobile assembly line, as our servants. Yet they are, as truly as the barber who cuts our hair or the woman who comes in by the day to help with the family washing.

Service does things to those who are served. A young woman was once overheard interviewing a prospective employee in an agency for domestic help. She wanted some one to begin work as soon as possible. Did the prospect think that she could be at a given address, with all her belongings, ready to stay, at twelve o'clock? (The interview took place fairly late in the morning.) No? Why not? Could she be there at one? At two? She could? Well, the young woman herself would not be there. She would leave the keys with the doorman. No one had been in the apartment all summer. It must be thoroughly cleaned, the necessary shopping done (she would leave a menu and the addresses of her tradesmen), and dinner for four people prepared by seven o'clock.

The lack of consideration displayed here is something more than careless indifference. It is an insensitivity which develops all too easily when one is habitually served. One comes to accept service without considering the individual who renders it. We are particularly prone to accept without question or consideration the services that are essential. We must eat, and so the person who cooks the food is often unthinkingly exploited. Perhaps this also accounts for the fact that the doctor, who serves us in such an essential capacity, is often forgotten when the bills are paid. This easy acceptance of essential services is a first step toward intolerance. For one can not be really concerned about understanding the people one exploits, be that exploitation thoughtless or calculated. Here rises a barrier that, once created, may later be the basis for active intolerance.

Intolerance toward those with a different background of social traditions springs more from the community climate of opinion than from individual reactions. When a homogeneous community becomes established, any element which differs from it is regarded as suspect. The good citizens of Philadelphia were very glad to send the immigrants from Germany and the Low Countries who came after them to the New World farther on into western Pennsylvania. They felt more comfortable having these people, who spoke a different language and worshiped in a different church, at some distance from themselves. Long before the Revolution they took the first steps toward limiting immigration by stipulating to the companies who brought these people over in their boats how many were to be accommodated at one time.

This community feeling toward the outlander is often

deep-seated historically. On the European continent, where successive waves of population have succeeded each other from the days of pre-history on, the origins of these communal feelings about other people are all but lost, yet the feelings themselves may still be strong enough to destroy us all. No one is very clear about why a Czech and a German can not live comfortably side by side, but the feeling is fairly common on both sides that they "just can't." Only an exhaustive study of the history of both Teutons and Slavs could trace the reasons for those feelings with any certainty.

America is preëminently fortunate in that she can shake these historic hang-overs if she will. Immigrants from every country, from every small racial group, can live together here, and do, without violating any of the proprieties. For this reason we are fortunately placed to take advantage of the best in all cultures. Every racial group, every religious sect, every family tradition can make its contribution. But conditions within a community must be favorable in order to have this take place. There must be receivers as well as givers when contributions are made. If we try to absorb these groups indiscriminately, spreading over them all an established Anglo-Saxon pattern of conformity, much is lost.

Just how far an established community should go in welcoming patterns of living different from its own is not an easy question to decide. However, if we keep an open mind about the outlander, recognize his differences as well as his similarities, and do not measure his worth merely by his ability to conform, we are likely to find that he has

We must try to understand other people, not only as human beings but as human beings with a distinct and worth-while cultural background. Here American children and a Chinese boy find a common interest helpful to better understanding.

much to contribute which will enrich our own community living without in any way disrupting its basic design. In the early days of President Roosevelt's administration, there was a scheme on foot to build up communities for workers on largely cultural lines, communities to be built around the social, as well as the economic, needs of people of different cultural backgrounds. The task was colossal and soon fell through. But the idea behind it was sound. When more of us try to understand the needs of other people, not only as human beings but as human beings with a distinct and worth-while cultural background, something of this kind may materialize. If it does, it will make a considerable contribution toward that integration we need so badly. There is a good deal to be said for roots, cultural or otherwise.

There is still another group of people toward whom intolerance is often shown. These people do not necessarily belong in one economic group. They do not have a common racial or cultural heritage. It is their behavior that sets them apart. Attitudes toward these people are perhaps the most difficult of all to define. Anti-social behavior covers a wide range—all the way from the divorcee to the sexual pervert, from the juvenile delinquent to the criminally insane. It includes under the same indiscriminating head the swindler, the social revolutionary, the exponent of nudism or free love. We feel, almost instinctively, that any very strange behavior or idea threatens our own comfortable way of living. Some of these people obviously do endanger society. Even so, we must go beyond blind intolerance in our attitude.

There are two main reasons why we fail to do so. Either we consider the established way of doing things to be an absolute, the only way because it is the way that we are used to; or else we consider the behavior which offends us a mere perversity, indulged in by some one who could behave more acceptably if he would. But to-day's fund of knowledge modifies both these views. Descriptions of other societies often give us a critical bird's-eye view of our own. With more explorations into individual psychology, into the effects of environment on character, into the connections between disease and crime, we can get a much better perspective on why people behave the way they do.

The more we know, the more we realize that no true and fair judgment of behavior can be made without a comprehensive study of each particular case. The reasons for some anti-social behavior may be found in the faults of the social structure itself. Others may be purely personal in character. Most behavior, though, whether it is actually anti-social or merely "queer," is a combination of the two.

If we judge such behavior without attempting to understand its motivation, we set up a barrier of intolerance. In this case, such a barrier shuts the door to possible guides that might help us in the improvement of both society and people. Nudism as practised may be silly, but its back-to-nature origin is, to some extent, sound. Stealing is a crime in our society, yet it often dramatically shows up social injustice, or throws into relief the undue emphasis which is put upon money values. We do not have to condone anti-social, or even asocial, behavior, but we must be ready to understand it. We must also learn not to make blanket condemnations when we are in no position to understand.

II

A Child's Attitude toward the People Who Serve Him

THE TOLERANCE WE WANT OUR CHILDREN TO GROW INTO is more than a passive live-and-let-live affair. It has a positive, constructive aspect. It is an alert and sensitive awareness of human beings, of their needs and hopes and potentialities. It is a sympathetic understanding of their foibles and their backslidings. It is an ability to see the person behind the façade of class or race or behavior, however obtrusive or dramatic such a façade may be.

Tolerance begins at home. Children imitate behavior long before they understand it. This is especially true of the behavior that is outside their own immediate concerns. Relationships between adults are not easy for a child to comprehend. He therefore takes his cue on how to treat other people chiefly from what he sees and hears about him. If he sees servants within the home being treated with consideration and kindliness, he will be friendly toward them also. If he overhears talk of undesirable neighbors, he will the more readily join a neighborhood gang in ridiculing a child with dark skin or a queer-sounding name. If we do not want him to acquire an insensitive shell early, we must be sure that we ourselves are blameless. But this is only the beginning. There are many concrete, considered things that we can do to further a tolerant attitude toward other people.

We have stressed before how important a sympathetic and coöperative attitude toward those who serve us is if we are to revitalize and give meaning to the complex, dependent way in which we live. Such an attitude begins at home, although it can not end there. Unless the groundwork for it is laid in home life, tolerance may never go deeper than words.

A young college graduate, enthusiastic in the cause of labor, was on the way home from a conference on social relationships. The taximan who drove her group to the railroad station had defective brakes and dared not drive fast enough to reach the station in the short time his passengers had allowed themselves. The young woman made many remarks upon that drive. She never once addressed the driver directly. She talked about his delinquency as if he were merely an appendage of the machine, incapable of hearing or feeling. Her enthusiasm for laborers as a class did not prevent her from being insensitive toward the person who was serving her at the moment. The reason for this inconsistency may well have been that this girl was brought up in a household where service was largely taken for granted, where the personalities of servants did not often intrude themselves into the picture.

Being served makes one insensitive to the rights of those who do the serving, unless this very thing is guarded against. This is not only true of paid service, of course. There are classic examples of it in the spoiled child whose mother waits on him hand and foot, in the proverbial spoiled husband or selfish wife. In any of these cases, respect for the person who does the running and consideration of his rights or needs dwindle as the demands increase.

Children are not capable of guarding themselves against this penalty of service. They do not have the objectivity in regard to their own behavior nor the insight into the needs of others necessary for this. Therefore, it is up to us to do it for them. It is up to us to keep them aware of the person who performs the service, and aware of their own indebtedness.

The attitudes of children toward those who serve them directly. Small children are peculiarly placed in respect to service. Every one serves them, and acceptance of that fact forms a necessary stability beneath their feet. The members of a household who contribute to a small child's comfort are all near and dear to him. The baby who, like a small animal, associates his comfort with his best-beloved often shows an embarrassing preference for the nurse who cares for him. The small child, then, has a perfectly natural emotional affiliation with those who serve him, before he is aware of social distinctions at all. If we handle the situation skilfully, there is no reason why such distinctions should overlay what is desirable in this natural emotional response. Instead, it can be made the basis for a wider understanding and sympathy as he matures.

If some one besides his mother has the major care of a small child, questions of relative authority sometimes come up. It is important on several counts that a child have no doubts about the authority of the person who has direct responsibility for him. If such doubts exist about an employed person, even a little child will be quick to sense his advantage and make capital of it.

Almost any person who has been employed in a number of families as nurse or governess has had some experience of this kind. The dilemma may be a very perplexing one. It may, in extreme cases, come to humoring a child against one's better judgment or losing one's job. Even short of this, the sense that one's decisions may be countermanded is no help in making them. With a nurse undecided as to what to ask of children, and children recognizing that indecision, we can not expect much of the relationship. To give children such power over another person is one of the best ways of defeating our ends. For no one can respect a person whom he can manipulate at will. It is well for the mother and the nurse to get together beforehand on what a general policy shall be. Any differences that come up later had better be discussed in private. A lot of trouble can often be avoided by making ends and aims clear from the start.

One mother, herself employed and seldom at home, worked out a scheme whereby her information about what went on there was not left entirely to chance. She asked Mathilde, who was with the children all day, to make a note of any difficulties that arose. Twice a week she managed to get home early enough to have a talk about

these with her. Over a cup of tea, with it clearly understood that Mathilde and Mother were busy and were
not to be disturbed, they had a chat together about what
was going on. Mathilde explained how she had managed
certain situations, and the children's mother approved or
made clear her disagreement. Together they worked out
future procedure.

One must, of course, have complete confidence in the
integrity of the person employed to take care of one's
children if relations are to be satisfactory. Such a person
must also be capable of understanding, as well as willing
to carry out, the family point of view.

Sometimes it is hard for a little child to keep the proper
perspective when there is one person who always seems
to be at his beck and call. If the three-year-old is used to
seeing his mother busy about other things, if his demands
are sometimes met with, "You will have to wait until I
get through here, I'm busy now," he comes to realize that
his desires are not always the most important consideration. If, however, there is some one always ready to help
him, he will not readily get that sense. He is quite likely
to become unreasonable in his demands. After all, why
shouldn't Annie pick up the clothes he strews about, or
the pieces of paper that fall on the floor when he cuts out
pictures? She doesn't seem to have anything else to do.

Of course, just because there is some one whose only
job is to take care of him, a child should not shirk his
own responsibilities. Taking care of his own things, doing
his own picking up to a large extent, doing a lot toward
dressing and washing himself, are all to be expected of

the three-year-old. Such duties are part of his growing up. Sometimes one has to impress this fact upon his nurse, however. It is often easier for her, as well as for him, if she does these things for him.

For both these reasons, a small child's responsibilities have to be thought out beforehand. In his own best interest, he should be expected to do whatever he can by himself. In the best interests of every one, he should not be allowed to make unnecessary demands on other people. Nurse, too, can find occasion to be "busy." Even if she is mainly occupied in watching what goes on, a piece of sewing, writing materials, or a book can occupy her attention enough so that Johnny is forced to realize that his concerns are not the only ones that count.

The attitudes of children toward those who serve the home. Young William's mother was attracted to the kitchen by sounds. William, it seemed, was laying down the law. His tone of voice was anything but pleasant. "I don't want you to touch my things," she heard him declare. On inquiring what was the matter, she discovered that Mary, the new cook and general helper, had been cleaning in William's room, and William was objecting to the results. "She's only the cook, and she doesn't know anything. I won't have her mixing up my things," he announced. His mother was genuinely shocked. This was not the way she wanted William to feel; not at all. Whatever had brought about such sentiments?

The reason for William's ideas about cooks was not hard to find, once his mother gave it some thought. For some time she had been having difficulties in finding satisfactory help. One unsatisfactory arrangement had followed another, and there had been much discussion on the subject, some of which William had necessarily overheard. He had formed his ideas accordingly. The frequent changes had given him little opportunity to know any of these people; they remained for the most part strangers, "persons who didn't know anything."

William's mother did a lot of thinking that night. Her conclusions were announced at breakfast. For a few weeks, at least, she was going to give up haunting agencies and do her own work. Whenever the opportunity offered, William was going to help. Perhaps if he were about a kitchen more and helped a little with its work, he would find out that cooking was a worth-while and interesting, as well as a necessary, job. This might help him to have more respect for cooks.

The presence of servants in a home is often a problem requiring much thought, for the best family living is a coöperative affair. Mutual assistance and consideration are basic in its design. If servants are employed, they should share these privileges, too. This means, of course, that those we employ must be people with whom children can associate freely. They must also be capable of understanding, at least in part, what family objectives are and be willing to do their share toward achieving them. Such qualifications are just as important as an ability to cook or a clean bill of health.

If the household is not too highly organized, children themselves can be expected to help in keeping its routine

The grocery clerk, the butcher's delivery boy, the laundry collector can often be friendly acquaintances as well as familiar figures.

going. Some of their jobs can be under the supervision of the specialists. Cook may be a better instructor than Mother in the art of making cream sauce. The young gardener or mechanic may get valuable hints from the practical common sense of the man who helps with odd jobs. Respect for the person who knows how to do something well is a sound basis for any relationship.

The question that comes to mind in this connection is: how much unskilled help and interested meddling will busy people tolerate? Cooks are notoriously finicky about who messes around in their kitchens, and paid help is quite likely to be wary of children. The answer to this, however, depends largely on the children themselves. If youngsters have been helped to develop good social habits, and if relationships with employees are on a good footing all around, these chances of worth-while apprenticeship will often develop naturally with a little encouragement.

There are also specific things we can do to emphasize for children the personality of the people around them. Appreciation of some of their preferences helps. One little boy quite proudly presented his "Anna" with a small bunch of violets bought out of his own hoarded pocket-money. He knew that she liked violets, because she had told him stories of how she and her brothers and sisters had picked them when they were children and lived in the country. The initial suggestion for this thoughtful gift came from his mother, but the enthusiastic planning and carrying out of the idea were entirely his.

Some understanding of the personal relationships and responsibilities of these people is also a help in realizing them as personalities. The fact that Mrs. Rooney, who came in three times a week to clean house and do the laundry, had a little boy, too, came as quite a surprise to Jimmy. Who took care of the little boy while she was away? Mrs. Rooney explained that Mr. Rooney was at home. Jimmy was very much interested in this arrangement, so different from the one familiar to him. At Christmas time it was Jimmy himself who thought of buying a bright red automobile, like the one he treasured, for Mrs. Rooney's little boy, "whose Daddy took care of him."

The attitude of children toward servants outside the home. Consideration for, and understanding of, those who serve us can soon be extended beyond the confines of home. Children who live in apartments find helpful friends in the doorman and the man who runs the elevator. These people can be made real as personalities by courteous treatment and by being remembered in some special way occasionally. The discovery of mutual interests may also help. A ten-year-old who was proud of his stamp collection found an enthusiastic fellow-philatelist in the elevator boy of his apartment building. Then there are the delivery men who bring us our food, our clean clothes, our department-store purchases. These people come and go, and there is little opportunity to know them as individuals. However, those of us who live in the suburbs and habitually shop in the same stores do have the chance to personalize some of them. The grocery clerk, the butcher's delivery boy, the laundry collector can often be friendly acquaintances as well as familiar figures.

As children grow older some knowledge of the tasks involved in the familiar services that touch them nearest is a help in appreciating and understanding the people who do these tasks. Some information about the daily jobs of such people as the postman, the milkman, and the men who drive delivery trucks, some understanding of their responsibilities and duties, make them more real as people. To have in the back of one's mind the knowledge that the milkman whom one sees driving through the street was up before daybreak, that he has done his job and is now probably on his way back, to leave his truck and go home to an early dinner and an early bedtime, makes him a more interesting person than he might otherwise be. Without this information, one might not see the milkman at all.

Information about the many jobs that keep our industry and transportation functioning can be had in a number of ways. It can form interesting content for the family reading and the family trips. Always, however, we must be careful to make these things meaningful in terms of the people who are concerned. The trains, the ships, the machines of mine and factory are fascinating in themselves, but it is the people who operate them who are important.

III

A Child's Attitude toward People Who Are "Different"

How OFTEN AND HOW DEEPLY CHILDREN MAY NEED HELP in meeting strange people, we are prone to forget. When a child who is strange only to the extent of being "new" comes into a group of youngsters, he is apt to be rejected or even persecuted. If conspicuous differences of cultural background are involved, trouble is even more likely. There is no simple cure for all the uneasinesses that may be touched off by such an occasion. But certainly we can work to prevent their hardening into prejudices. This we can do day by day, not only when the problem looms up large.

Helping children appreciate cultural differences. If we are on the alert, many opportunities present themselves for helping children understand people of different backgrounds. Very often such contacts can begin right at home. The servants we employ often come from different countries. If one is fortunate enough to have such a direct contact, even a small child can begin to understand that there are other customs, other ways of living, besides his own. Children are naturally curious and easily intrigued by things that are different. There are many roads that lead out into the unknown. Folk-tales, pictures of the "old country," of native costumes and native festivals, the taste of native food may all be drawn upon to make the traditions of a Swedish maid or an Italian grocer more real.

One mother found her opportunity for extending boundaries in this way when an Italian family moved into the neighborhood. Dominick seemed strange to the other children because of his dark skin and halting speech. Six-year-old Jon, self-consciously precise in his articulation, could not help laughing at the queer sound of some of Dominick's words. By skilful questioning, Jon's mother found out from what part of Italy the little boy had come. The *National Geographic* yielded pictures of Dominick's village, its people, and its countryside. Later, Dominick's mother contributed some plants of basil and finocchi, so prized in Italian cooking, to Jon's vegetable plot. In such ways as this, not only Dominick but also the different background to which he belonged became more understandable to Jon.

An interest in immigrant groups, in their traditions and in what they have contributed to America, can be extended in many ways as children grow older. Some of this is, of course, done in our schools. But if we are alert to the opportunities offered by everyday living, we can add the flavor of immediacy and of personal interest to what might, left entirely to the schools, be merely an academic matter. As an interest in foreign countries grows, some connection can be made between them and the people who have come from them to live with us. The story about the little Swedish boy or the child of some faraway Central European country need not serve its whole purpose as an interesting story; it can help to make more graphic the problems of these people as immigrants. What happens to Olaf or Ignace when he comes, from the hills where he learned how to take care of the cows, to a big, bewildering city like New York? No wonder he is so silent and seems so strange. Why did he come, and how can the things he learned in Yugoslavia or Sweden be a help to him here, as well as a help to us? Such questions, and others like them, can help to further an understanding of people who are different from ourselves.

Family automobile trips also give an excellent opportunity for a better understanding of different ways of living. The differences between parts of our own country are immediately apparent to the traveler's eye. The tie-up between the geography of the land through which the motor-road runs and the way that people live, what they do for a living, how their towns are built, is not difficult to see. Even a late afternoon's stroll about the town in which one's overnight tourist home is located can answer many questions of this kind, as well as stretch cramped muscles. Our own land is rich in variety. Appreciation of this fact, as well as of the close connection between habitat and living, will give an added basis for understanding the differences of people who come from other lands.

Helping children to understand different behavior. Perhaps the most difficult people of all to interpret for children are those who are anti-social, who have trans-

A story about a child from some faraway country need not serve its whole purpose as an interesting story; it can help to make more graphic the problems of these people as immigrants.

gressed some social regulation. Four-year-old Danny was genuinely puzzled by the idea, newly acquired, that policemen have occasion to deal summarily with grown-ups. He had taken it for granted that a policeman's whole duty was concerned with keeping children off the grass in the park and helping them to cross the street. The fact that grown-ups, too, had to be corrected opened up an entirely new, and not an easy, field of speculation.

Sometimes, for their own safety, small children have to understand that all adults are not worthy of trust. There are quite different ways of giving them such understanding, and much depends upon how it is done. How can we give an explanation that can be grasped by a child and still leave an opening for more complete understanding later? We have already stated of what such mature understanding consists. It sees the behavior of the individual in relation to his innate capacity and to the environmental factors that have surrounded him. It does not accept anti-social behavior as inevitable, nor does it isolate it from the social context as a whole. Even first explanations should lay the basis for this kind of understanding.

In the first place, the ordinary precautions in regard to strangers can be put on a general, impersonal basis. One does not approach strangers. The policeman is the person to go to if one needs help. If a strange person speaks first, one is polite and friendly but not communicative. One never goes anywhere with a stranger alone. These things can be understood as among the "things that are done" and can be put on that basis so far as children are concerned. There does not need to be any aura of fear or suspicion to insure compliance.

The same emphasis can often be used in explaining other people's conduct, when this is necessary, as is used in speaking of a child's conduct. Much misconduct can be explained as a lack of understanding, as a momentary forgetfulness, or as a loss of self-control. All these are understandably familiar to children. That grown-ups, too, have these difficulties in self-discipline and have to be set right by some one else may be a new idea, as it was to Danny, but it is an idea that can be assimilated with fewer repercussions than one which arbitrarily classifies people who are anti-social as "bad."

The expression, "He didn't—or doesn't—understand," not only is intelligible, even to a little child, but it explains anti-social behavior in a way that ensures a more just appraisal of it later on. The person who habitually transgresses community laws does not understand their true import; the person who wrongs or hurts another does not understand, in any real sense, what such hurt or wrong means. He may not be capable of understanding. His own more immediate sense of wrong or need, his mental or emotional endowment, his previous experience, may prevent him from ever understanding. But if his behavior is seen in this light, the chances for its correction are immeasurably increased.

As a child's experiences with his peers widen, they can be used to illuminate the misbehavior of adults. In explaining a kidnapping to his eight-year-old son in terms of his own dearest possession, a pet rabbit, one father found himself confronted with this:

"But Daddy, if Billy took my rabbit because he wanted me to do something, it would be something he wanted very much, wouldn't it? No one would do a thing like that for just a little thing. Do people want money that much?"

Thus the way was open for some insight into the pressures that often lead to criminal acts. Many of these are understandable to children. Actual want they may never know, but the desire for certain things, or for the chance to shine in the reflected glory of a new possession, or to dispense largess to admiring associates, are known to them by experience.

There are certain things we must guard against in the attitudes of children toward anti-social persons. First, there is the attitude of fear. Sometimes this has to be dealt with, despite all our care in not letting it tinge ordinary caution. One little girl who had a good three-quarters of a mile to walk to school was exposed to a neighborhood "Jack-the-Ripper" scare. The scare was entirely unfounded, one of those unexplainable eruptions that sometimes occur. This was explained to her, as was also the tendency for stories of this kind to grow when told from mouth to mouth. The fact that her own parents were not affected and that she was expected to go to school as usual helped her to get the better of her fears. For a day or so, that walk was not pleasant. But she came through with a sense of having conquered a foolish notion, and there were no aftermaths. There might have been, if her incipient fears had been indulged.

The nine-year-old sometimes picks up a sense of glamour in regard to persons who are habitually outside the law. The adventurous character of their deeds appeals to his love of action and daring. On the other hand, the thrill of the chase has its glamour, too. We must be sure that his concepts of anti-social behavior go beyond this. Thinking of anti-social persons either as knights in disguise or as hunted creatures does not make for better understanding. "Gangsters" must not only be persons whose deeds are exciting or whom it is exciting to "capture"; even the nine-year-old can begin to see these people in terms of their background and of the incongruities of community life. Literature may be a help here. Such a story as *Oliver Twist*, for instance, edited to hold his interest, will do a lot to clear up the connections between crime and circumstance. This is not easy ground, to be sure. We may have to feel our way carefully. But the important thing is to realize that it is ground that should be explored as soon as the need arises.

Older children become increasingly conscious of the social context out of which many criminal acts grow. Soon after the Lindbergh kidnapping, a company that manufactures fencing had a full-page advertisement in a prominent daily newspaper. It pictured a large residence surrounded by spacious lawns and securely closed by a high wire fence. On the lawn several children and a dog were playing. Outside the fence a man and a woman, old, ill-clad, and carrying clumsy bundles, were seen walking by.

A group of junior high school youngsters was given this picture to discuss. A most interesting half-hour followed. Many questions were raised. Was the fencing company justified in leaving the impression that all ill-clad people were suspect? If so, wasn't it time to do something about poverty? One youngster said he was glad he wasn't rich, if he would have to be afraid, too. Another said he thought that the fence might make people on the outside who were cold and hungry all the madder and set them to planning ways of getting in. So the talk went, far beyond the implications obviously intended by the picture. Such discussions can be very fruitful indeed, at home as well as at school.

In a truly democratic society, one functions *with* other people. People are judged primarily by their functioning. An attitude of tolerance and understanding makes acting together possible. True tolerance is the impetus from which a democratic community springs.

V

The Outside Community World

I

Community Living

WITH ALL OUR TALK OF DEMOCRACY, THERE HAS ALWAYS been a curious inconsistency in its practice. A government which has been termed representative has in practice been regarded as something quite apart from the individual it represents. All too frequently it is regarded as something beneath his respect. If we are to strengthen the underpinnings of the democratic ideal, such an attitude will have to be changed. We will have to develop a much more realistic concept of what democracy is and build this meaning much more firmly into our personal lives.

In theory, a democracy is a coöperating political unit. From the first, however, there has been some vagueness as to the sphere of democratic government. This vagueness was doubtless intentionally written into the Constitution by the men who framed it, and rightly so. For the functions of a government by the people must change as the people change in their living conditions and needs. Our mistake lies not in extending the functions of government, but in divorcing ourselves, in our community life, from those functions. The most essential feature of democratic government is that it is not imposed from a periphery, but rather proceeds from the center outward, in ever-increasing circles, and always with a communal organization simple enough and real enough at its core to be actually participated in by every individual. So conceived, its functioning is the functioning of the community, its scope the compass of communal life. It must have been their recognition of this expanding nature of coöperative government which caused our early political leaders to declare politically the individual rights of "life, liberty, and the pursuit of happiness."

Though they were keenly aware of the implications of the government they were inaugurating, those early leaders were not in so fortunate a position as ourselves for carrying them out. Our modern conquest of time and space has given us a distinct advantage, making possible, as it does, direct and instantaneous contact with all sections of a sprawling country. When it took weeks for news of affairs in the capital to travel to those sections most vitally concerned, when contacts were infrequent and uncertain, it was only natural that the government itself should seem as remote as its geographical position. To-day, when a turn of the dial puts many homes in direct contact with the legislature, when the substance of its deliberations is available almost as soon as it is written into the record, our chances of effecting a working integration as real as this physical one ought to be immeasurably increased. There are, however, considerable stumbling-blocks in the way.

Some characteristics of our communities. By derivation, the word *community* signifies a group of individuals who live under the same conditions and who, by mutually sharing services and resources, maintain a common existence. This is not the picture that voluntarily comes up in one's mind, however. Actual communities are quite different.

Consider, for instance, a hypothetical small town in the truck-farming part of New Jersey. The bulk of its money would be made by the sale of vegetables to the metropolitan areas of New York and Philadelphia. Most of the workers in its fields would come and go as harvests occurred. They would draw wages which, for the most part, would be spent in other sections. Some of its local food stores would belong to national chains and be managed and partly staffed by people from other places. The profits from these stores would go back to a central office in New York. Local recreation would center chiefly about a movie house showing nationally distributed films. In addition, there would be the radios, whose programs are also aimed at a wide and diffuse audience. Regular bus services would run to both New York and Philadelphia. A train service would bring both these cities near enough for a day's shopping; or, if one did not mind late hours, an evening's entertainment. The Grange and the Methodist church in this town might very well find their active workers dwindling and many of their meetings poorly attended. The local fire department and the local school might both suffer from lack of funds.

Such a town would be, in spite of its close connections with urban areas, predominantly rural in character. Matters are even more amorphous when one looks closely at communities within the metropolitan areas themselves. In communities that depend chiefly upon the city for employment, goods, and recreation there is little besides a few struggling churches, a women's club, or a civic organization to mark community bounds. And the city itself? Settlement houses and church community centers try valiantly to give their neighborhoods character, to give them an integral being to which people can feel that they belong. Consumer coöperative clubs are also stepping into the breach. But the moving-van makes all such efforts discouraging. The populations of rooming-houses and of apartment buildings have little cohesion. Although their character may be constant in any one neighborhood, their individual membership is usually not the same for long.

An increasingly large part of our population finds it advantageous to "travel light," to change residence often and to strike few roots. Transient labor and the roving unemployed make up a part of this number. But the shifts of office personnel, of construction officials and the like, which large industrial concerns find necessary, also contribute to it. Then there is the unattached group which takes to trailers and winters in Florida. None of these people belong, in any real sense of the word, to a community. Wherever they are, a community goes on around them. They take no responsibility for it.

The uniformity that tends to draw all community living into the urban pattern, to level out differences, also helps to blur community lines. When one Main Street looks very much like another, it makes little difference to which one belongs. When every small town is trying to act like a city, one might just as well go to the city and have the real thing.

This loss of community character and cohesion is the other side of the encouraging picture we drew a moment ago. The same changes that make possible a more real national community tend to pull smaller groups apart. Neighborhood life has often become amorphous for the same reason that family life has—because the materials of living are supplied at long range and from the outside. There is not enough local functioning to hold the group together.

True, there are forces that operate in other directions. The growing emphasis on regional cultures, the community character of some housing developments, the experiments in genuine community living that the depression instigated, the emphasis of some educational work done by farm organizations—all these are encouraging straws in the wind. But their influence is as yet limited.

Why community emphasis is important. Democratic procedure presupposes community responsibility. Yet no one can really feel responsible for something that has only a hypothetical existence for him. To have meaning, the sense of community must be in some measure a daily and intimate experience. It is the local community to which one belongs in this immediate, active way. If this community remains unreal, external, there is little chance that the larger social groupings, the coördinating units of state and nation, will have much meaning, either, no matter how easily we can communicate with one end of our land from the other.

Evidences that communities have little real meaning for many people are all about us. Government taxes are dodged while government services are used. Government enterprise is ridiculed while we live by its fruits. One sees the same thing in smaller, but no less significant, ways. A city's water supply is thoughtlessly wasted; the benches in a city park or subway station are defaced; school books belonging to a city's schools are heedlessly mutilated.

All this behavior, from the magnate's subterfuge to escape the income tax to the ten-year-old youngster's careless use of his new geography textbook, is the result of the same thing. What belongs to you and me and a number of other people belongs to nobody unless you and I—and the other people—have a personal sense of belonging together to a functioning social group. This sense is hard to achieve in communities such as we have been describing. Moreover, we have, to some extent, deliberately minimized it.

When the Moscow subway system was opened, there were newspaper stories in this country stressing the pride and individual sense of ownership that people felt toward it. The opening of New York's Independent subway system, also owned by a municipal unit, brought forth no such comment. Yet New York's Independent subway is just as much a communal service as is the Russian system. It is to Soviet advantage to stress communal ownership. Our own situation makes such emphasis difficult.

Why is the community emphasis so hard to make?

The history of our public utilities is illuminating in this connection. Roads, water supply, transportation facilities —all have gone through much the same history. At first they were owned by private companies for the profits to be derived from them. When, because of overlappings of one kind or another, or because of the extension of operation necessary, these services became either unprofitable or unsatisfactory, they were taken over by the community. Thus, public utilities have, to a large extent, a privately owned past. By the time they come under public control, every one is used to the services they render and little thought is given to their changed status.

Other services go through a slightly different history but with similar results. Hospitals, libraries, social organizations, even schools usually begin under private auspices. They are run first of all as philanthropies, ways to spend for the public good the money that has been taken out of the community, or out of other communities, in profits. Here, too, government responsibility is a late comer. By the time it steps in to carry on what has become an indispensable service, the flavor of charity, of special dispensation, has left its indelible mark.

Such a history has some advantages. The roads might not have come so quickly, nor the libraries have been considered indispensable so soon, if individuals had not forged ahead on their own. But it has its penalties, too. It leads to an acceptance of communal services without any real awareness of what they imply. One grumbles about the subway that is city-owned as one did about the one that was run privately, without once considering that now one has some measure of responsibility in the matter. Used to the condescension of privately owned institutions, one comes to think that the city hospital, too, is a place where people may "get something for nothing."

A sense of responsibility in community life is also hampered by the contradictions and incongruities within our communities. The line between services that are privately run and those which are performed by the community is a constantly wavering one. It also varies widely from one community to the next. One city may have several transport lines, some privately owned, some municipal. One town may own a municipal power-plant. Its neighbor twenty miles away may vote down a similar project as "communistic." Food and clothing are universally considered to be matters for private handling, yet surplus commodities are dispensed by the government to those who need them. In many places the expense of low-cost housing is being undertaken by the government for the same reason that it undertook the building of roads—because the job is too involved and too expensive for private hands.

No matter how much a community undertakes to do for itself, however, the emphasis rarely changes. Privately owned businesses are still in the foreground, and each necessary step toward communal responsibility is deprecated and deplored. Little is heard about the many worthwhile government services that are functioning well. Perfectly geared machinery runs quietly. There is usually enough well-geared machinery in any community to make

Social functioning can be real and important to children. This group, getting out a school paper, has made its own analysis of the way in which its community functions.

its citizens proud, to give them an incentive toward making more of it run well. But it is the sputtery kind that gets the publicity.

Our major problem in the years to come will be to make our democracy a functioning reality in the face of these handicaps. This is a task that must be attempted on many fronts, of course. But it is one that has a peculiar significance for those of us who are particularly concerned with the welfare of individuals and of families. In glancing back on what we have been saying about the necessity for belonging to a community, one may well have a question in mind. Totalitarian states put a lot of emphasis on belonging, too; they rate community responsibility very high, so high that it overrides the rights of individuals altogether. In stressing community functioning, are we not in danger of doing the same thing?

The answer to this is implicit in our point of view. For so much depends on *who* does the stressing. If, as parents, we make the most of our opportunities, social functioning can be real and important to children. And if we do the job, the results will be quite different from those obtained in Germany, for instance, where it is done by administrators. The state may think in terms of unwieldy groups; families, of necessity, think in terms of individuals. When we give meaning to social functioning as parents, we do it in these terms. To us, what is important for individuals is important in communities, too. As parents, we think first of health, of happy activity, of intellectual and emotional growth. What is best for children becomes our criterion.

So long as parents interpret communities, there will be little danger of totalitarian emphasis. For to us the community exists so that individuals can grow, and not the other way around. Interpreting and giving meaning to community life, therefore, is preëminently our job.

II

Helping Children Explore Community Functioning

THE SENSE OF BELONGING IN A COMMUNITY COMES IN several different ways. One belongs through using, with awareness, the community's services; through appreciating its cultural and historical heritage; and, finally, through active social functioning, through doing things with other people. These ways of belonging apply to the large, coördinating units of state and nation as well as to one's own small neighborhood.

Exploring the present functioning of a community. Little children are immensely interested in the adult life that goes on around them. It is the activity of this life, the things people do, which fire their imaginations and engage their interests. The two-year-old trots about after his mother, imitating her acts. He dusts the furniture, sets an imaginary table, puts his dolls to bed, imitating not only procedure, but also the tricks of behavior, the mannerisms, that he observes. As soon as his boundaries begin to widen, a child imitates the activities of the street and the neighborhood, too. He fastens an imaginary hose to the fire-hydrant and flushes the dirt and dust from the gutter; he races his express wagon to an imaginary fire; he delivers the mail, the groceries, and the milk.

With a little forethought we can direct and encourage a child's spontaneous interest in the activities that go on around him. In this imitative play we have an excellent opportunity to familiarize children with community functioning. So far as results are concerned, the grocer is just as much a community servant as is the policeman or the fireman—that is, he supplies just as vital a community need. A child's first picture of community activity is not confused with distinctions beween public and private service. He can see the services that sustain him as a working whole. If he sees them first in this way, he will be able, later on, to deal more intelligently with some of the incongruities.

There are three ways in which we can help children build up this picture of community activity. We can be ready to give adequate explanations when these are demanded; we can take our children exploring, to find out more about the things that have caught their interest; and we can supply them with the materials that can best carry on imitative play, which is their way of thinking things through.

One must be careful, at first, not to press explanations too far. It is better to keep the home end uppermost. The linemen are fixing wires so that *our* phone or light will work; the sewers are being fixed so that *our* sink or toilet will drain properly; the firemen are practising to be able more quickly to put out a fire on *our* street; the bakery

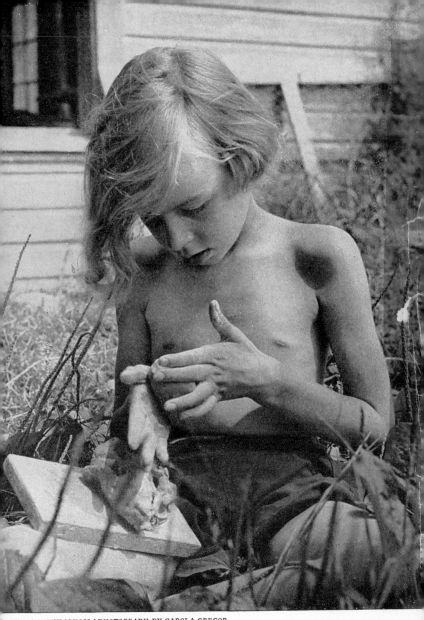

Re-creation expresses an active enjoyment of nature . . . Attempting to model a pet turtle or frog makes its essential individuality more vivid.

truck is delivering bread for *us* to buy. In this way, even the three-year-old can gain some conception of the many links that tie his home firmly to the community around it.

Further explanations, of course, will depend upon ability to understand. The four-year-old can grasp immediate happenings. He is also aware that some kind of sequence goes before, that the threads lead somewhere. His concept of sources, however, may be hazy. One little boy, who was on the consumer end of everything, had his own ideas about why the cow in the story his mother was reading did not have any more milk to give. Wise in the ways of gasoline trucks, filling-stations, and automobiles, he remarked, "The milk truck will have to fill her up again, won't it?" It takes more than picture-books and stories to straighten out such misconceptions. We must be careful not to rely too much on words; we must look for the opportunity actually to explore some of these remoter ends.

Just as the underlying relationships that determine a natural environment open out gradually for children, so the network of social connections is apparent to them only in pieces. It is up to us to help them fit the pieces together. Ordinary day-to-day happenings provide any number of starting points. One can begin wherever action of any kind makes functioning evident and dramatic. A trip to the grocer may coincide with the arrival of a supply truck; one can take a walk past the fire-house while drill is going on; or past a place where sewer pipes or electric wires are being repaired. Wherever people are doing things and whenever what they are doing can be grasped, it is well to stop and watch. It is really very annoying to be hurried past these interesting performances when one is four. We can remember this and allow extra time for watching.

Often an isolated happening can be linked in some way with other events; we can carry the thread a little farther, trace some familiar sight a little nearer to its source. Here are a few explorations of this kind that one mother undertook with her two youngsters, one of six and one of four.

A visit to the coal yard. A delivery of coal had been made to the children's home. Watching the black lumps hurtle down the chute and through the cellar window had been a fascinating experience. The coal had come in two loads, and the children naturally asked where the truck went to get the second one. Mother called the coal yard and arranged for a visit when freight cars would be unloading. In this way, two steps away from home, involving two kinds of transport, were accounted for.

A visit to the gasoline storage tanks. Soon after the coal-yard exploration, a gasoline truck happened to be supplying the underground tank at a filling-station when the children and their mother stopped there. This performance was worth watching, too. Danny wanted to know where this truck came from. The gasoline storage tanks were down near the river, not very far away. So a visit to these was arranged. Here the children saw the oil tankers come down the river, bringing supplies by water.

A visit to a bakery. Several times in succession, Danny, Mildred, and their mother went shopping early enough to see the day's supplies piled up in front of the grocery store. These boxes interested the children very much. One day they arrived in time to see a bakery truck unload its baskets of bread. It suddenly occurred to the children's mother that here was something that might be traced to its source without much difficulty. There was a bakery in town, small enough so that the processes would be intelligible. Before they went to see how one made many loaves of bread, however, some exploring was done at home to find out how one loaf was made. The machine-mixing and other processes were much easier to follow after one knew something about bread-making one's self.

A visit to a sand-bank. There was a new house going up not far from where the children lived. First the steam-shovel biting a hole and then the trundling and grumbling of trucks had made the street an exciting place. Soon the trucks began to come loaded instead of empty. Bricks and lumber began to arrive. The cement truck arrived, too. This was particularly popular because of its turning body and the way the thick, sticky mixture poured out. Indeed, the cement truck was so popular that one Saturday morning, when the children's father was home, they got out the car and followed it. Down by the river they discovered the place where the truck drove under two huge hoppers to be filled. They discovered the barges that brought in the sand and cement. They saw the tug that had just brought in a long line of sand barges with their load. All this was so fascinating that it led to another trip on the next Saturday, an all-day trip with a picnic lunch. Up the river some miles was a large sand-bank. Here they saw the barges loaded. They saw the sand being dug out by steam-shovels, put through huge sifters, and carried on a long conveyor belt, away from the sifters, under the road, and out to the waiting barge. On top of the bank trees and grass were growing, and from here one could see all the busyness below, while eating the picnic lunch.

All communities offer opportunities of this kind. The special treats of childhood do not all need to be connected with the circus or the zoo. These industrial performances can be just as interesting and more usable. For explanations and observations are only part of these experiences. After one sees something done, one wants to do it. At four, one wants to make believe, to play the experience through. This is the small child's way of making sure of it, of getting it straight in his mind. With the proper materials, these community experiences offer rich play content. As part of his play, they become a real part of his life.

The three-year-old who plays milk man needs only a toy truck or express wagon to go from house to house. When he wants to go farther—bring the milk from the country by train, get it bottled, and then deliver it—he can manage better on a smaller scale. Blocks that can be built into the train tracks, the bottling plant, and the houses are useful to him then. They can even serve for the trains and the trucks he will need. When we want children to expand their play in this way, blocks are a necessity in the play-room. The small representative toys

—the trains, cars, doll figures, and so on—that one can use with blocks are a help, too.

All the trips described above appeared in some form on the play-room floor. Here a coal yard was built, and a lively play went on that reproduced the delivery to the yard and then to houses, and, as a further touch, to stores. Here the river was marked out, and gasoline tanks were built along the shore. Farther on, the docks where the sand barges came in and the hoppers where the cement truck was filled appeared in block form. On another day a large bakery occupied Mildred's attention, and Danny was the storekeeper who sold her loaves of bread.

By keeping an eye on this kind of play, one can get a line on the pictures that children have of their social surroundings. There will be gaps and misconceptions. As much as possible, these should be filled out and corrected by more trips, more observation. Thus, gradually, through using the activities around him as content for his play, a child will become familiar with the workings of the community in which he lives.

As children grow older, the explorations they make can be extended to take in more complicated performances. While they are still reliving these experiences, they must be simple enough to be reproduced. The eight-year-old, however, does not rely so heavily on this method of assimilation. He can draw on a wider experience to reconstruct imaginatively and interpret what he sees. He can also use books to better advantage. A more detailed exploration of the way in which services work and of their many tie-ups with other places can then extend his information.

A power-plant, a municipal disposal plant, the railroad yards, where so many things come and go—all these deserve attention. A community's producing activities, if it has any, can also be explored to advantage. What the factories make, where their raw materials come from, why they are located here, who works in them, where their produce goes—the answers to these questions enlarge one's concepts of the community.

Learning active community responsibility. One must know about the services that contribute to community living in order to share in them consciously; but there is a responsibility to be shared, too. Children can be given a sense of participating, of sharing responsibility in a number of ways. Parents have a particular obligation here: school groups may visit around in a community enough to learn of its facilities, but only at home can children be given a real sense of responsibility. It is too much a piece of daily happenings to be adequately built at school.

Even the pre-school youngster can consciously play his community rôle. It begins in such small but important ways as keeping his wheel-toys off the sidewalk, not throwing papers on the street, helping Mother wrap the garbage into a compact, easily handled bundle, helping Daddy clear away the snow or rake up the leaves. These are among the things that are done, or not done, as a matter of course. But the reasons are important. Wheel-toys are kept off the sidewalk not only because that is the way one takes care of them, but also because the sidewalk belongs to every one, and it is up to us to keep our part of it in shape

Wherever a child's activity touches a community service, he can be made aware of his responsibility. Waiting for a policeman's whistle before crossing the street is a matter of safety; but it is a social obligation, too.

for every one to use. The garbage is handled in certain ways because we have a responsibility in this matter of disposal.

Wherever a child's activity touches a community service, he can be made aware of that fact and of the responsibility attached to his end. Waiting for a policeman's whistle or a green light before crossing the street is a matter of safety; but it is a social obligation, too, as it makes things easier for the people who drive automobiles. One does not pick up toys merely to keep the lawn looking neat; this neatness also helps to keep the street orderly. Leaving the tap in the bathroom running is not simply careless; it needlessly wastes water which we all use and which it is costing us all a lot to procure.

As a child's experience with public facilities widens, his sense of social responsibility grows. However, a lot depends on the uses that we expect him to make of them. We may expect too much. To the five-year-old, a museum corridor, for instance, may seem far more attractive for its unobstructed space than for the cases along its sides or the pictures on its walls. Used rightly, a museum is a repository of community culture to which one turns for information or enjoyment. In order to use it thus, one must know beforehand what one wishes to see and why one wishes to see it. The five-year-old can not use a museum in this way; therefore he is likely to misuse it. The same holds true for other facilities of this kind. We can help children to value these places as communal possessions by following this rule of use. The child who has some idea why he wishes to visit the museum will also know enough not to abuse the privilege.

III

Helping Children Explore a Community's Past

As CHILDREN GROW OLDER, EXPLORATIONS OF A COM-
munity's past can extend the picture they have been
building from their observations in the present. The
seven-year-old begins to speculate about "then" as well
as "now." How did people travel when there were no automobiles? What happened when fast trains did not bring
vegetables to the city? When there were no electric wires,
where did lights come from? Many such questions begin
to crop up. The seven-year-old has acquired enough first-
hand information to branch out. The more he discovers
about how grown-ups behave, how things are done, the
more he is able to reconstruct imaginatively out of book
material and other abstract sources the life of another
time.

Exploring the past history of a community gives one an
added sense of belonging. School programs have often
recognized this in connection with national history. The
history teacher has frequently been charged with a patriotic
mission. Explorations of local history can develop this
sense of belonging in an even more immediate and telling
way. Some school programs are beginning to realize this.

No matter what goes on at school, however, it is worth while for families to do some exploring of this kind on their own. For here, too, as in so many other things, the less formal, more spontaneous, kind of exploration that children and parents can do together has its advantages.

Exploring local geography. Human history, like the history of any other living thing, is largely based on habitat. The geography of a place, its physical make-up and its relation in space to other places, does much to determine its history. Discovering the natural layout of any community gives one a sure link by which the present may be fastened to the past. One can explore much geography on foot, and more of it in the family car. Even a young child begins to get an idea of the lay of the land about him. He picks up a lot of "geography" without realizing it. By deliberately exploring the physical characteristics of a community, these details of daily observation can be underlined.

It may be that the physical characteristics of another place have been the deciding factor in the development of a community. The growth of a city, itself a port, may overshadow in importance much surrounding territory. It may be that markets far away exert their influence, too. But the river whose bend makes a natural junction from which to send on the goods of the hinterland; the flat lands which used to support cattle and now grow grain; the mountains whose streams used to yield water-power and are now a city's playground; the terminal moraine, whose farms used to feed a city, that now provides suburban room for its homes—all these are sure threads into the past.

A sense of geography has its beginnings in an attempt to visualize space orientations. The four-year-old, in his block play, makes some attempt at such orientation. If *our* house is here, the street where the stores are must be *here;* the road that one takes to the river is *here;* the river goes *this* way. Often in this way a crude attempt at a map appears on the play-room floor.

By the time he is six or seven, a youngster can visualize these space relationships in more abstract ways. If there is some workable material such as plasticene handy, he can experiment with a relief map to show the discoveries that have been made on trips. Some effort to reproduce what one has seen is always a help in sharpening observation. The flat land where the farms were was on *this* side of the road; but was the high bank that had the swallow's nests in it *here*, or *here?* Gradually working out a plan of territory that is familiar in this way is a great help in seeing the physical contours of one's community clearly.

If it is at all possible—and with America becoming more air-minded, the possibilities are increasing—there is no better way of grasping the physical layout of land than by seeing it from an airplane. However, it is wise to do a lot of exploring on foot or by car first. The air picture is too confusing unless one has a number of landmarks by which to recognize it.

The habit of making maps is a good one to encourage, for maps can always be used to portray graphically the information one acquires. A large-scale map of one's community or neighborhood is an interesting and usable wall decoration for the play-room. If an outline of this territory is clearly drawn on a piece of cork or composition board, details can be added and changed at will. Buildings, street diagrams, scenery, and so on can be drawn on paper and tacked into their proper place on the outline. At one time these can show the neighborhood as it is now; at another, the way it was in the memory of some older person; at another, how it looked at a remoter date. Such use of an outline map keeps ever-present the sense of historical continuity.

Exploring a community's past. A sense of continuity is especially useful if the present community in which one lives has little to mark it as an entity. Suburban communities that are being absorbed into the city pattern take on new meaning as one traces the changes that rapid transit, new roads, and the like have brought about. One such community, now within the rapid-transit zone of a large city, was supplying that city with truck produce twenty years ago; before that, it was fruit and milk that went to the urban market; and before that, wheat. These changes had been so rapid that there were people to whom one could talk who remembered when the milk cans had gone rattling into the city, and who had themselves risen before daybreak to drive in the truck loads of green vegetables. The picture of its changing relation to its grasping neighbor made this community "come alive" in a dramatic way for one child. The excavations for a new apartment house revealed a portion of the clay bed which, long ago, had supported an active pottery industry. Here, too, was a tangible link with the past. A sample of excavated material, worked up for use, was shaped into an ash tray and fired in Mother's oven, "to see if it would look like those old jugs." The laying of a new street revealed a section of the old "Shell Road," and new meaning was given to what had previously been only a name on a sign-post, as the shells themselves were exposed.

There are many sources that can be used in exploring the past of a community. Local libraries are always helpful. Historical societies can often put one in touch with interesting material. There is usually some older person who prides himself on being acquainted with local lore. In one community I know, the doctor who has practised there for well over half a century is immensely popular with the children who come to him for tales of "how things used to be." On his walks with them he points out old landmarks and always has some amusing anecdote that makes these places live again for the children who have to be told what a livery-stable was and how busy the towpath that still runs past the deserted canal used to be.

Wherever one is, sources of local history can be found, though sometimes they have to be searched for. The search may prove equally fascinating to an adult and to a child. There are many sources that children themselves can not use very well. But the material one collects can be the subject of family discussion, stories, and even family plays. One family of three children entertained their relatives from another part of the country on Thanksgiving

Day by putting on a short play built about an interesting incident in local history.

Through trips, through explorations into the past, through some active reworking of the information they accumulate, children can gradually add depth and perspective to that picture of a community which they begin to piece together as soon as they can imitate the sights they see. Having that picture clear, children gain a real sense of being part of something. For here is something tangible, a continuous, functioning entity in which they live and work and play, just as children lived and worked and played yesterday and the day before.

IV

Helping Children Take Part in Community Living

AN AWARENESS OF FUNCTION SERVES TO DEFINE ONE'S PLACE in a community. An awareness of continuity, of cultural and historical heritage, serves to define community lines. Together, these two lay the groundwork for the third and most important way in which one belongs socially. In a democracy, each one of us has a responsibility for changing and shaping the community, too. Through working together with other people we have the chance to do this.

The importance of participating actively in community life. Our communities depend upon the social participation of their members. But such activity is important for individuals as well. We know that individuals need a sense of security for their well-being. Within a family we can assure this security for children, can consciously build it up. The wider world of the community is a different matter, however. Here, even a small amount of exploration reveals incongruities and conflicts that are confusing.

There are streets in any community that are not as well kept as others, houses which show evident signs of needing repair, people whose clothing needs are apparent even to a small child. There are also hospitals, jails, and criminal-court buildings. If we rule these things out of consciousness, pass them by, we are not facing the realities of the community in which we live. Yet these things spell insecurity. Admitted, they may disrupt the safe little world that is built up at home. They are tolerable only if we are doing something about them.

Family contacts with community groups. In order that children may grow naturally into the wider social responsibility that acts through groups, the family must have group contacts. Of course, all families do; but sometimes we do not use to best advantage the opportunities they offer. Particular thought deserves to be given the community groups with which a family is associated, in order that through them we may give children a sense of community participation. Some of them are better suited than others to this purpose.

A father's job can often be an important means of helping all members of the family to think of themselves as taking active part in the life of a community. If Father is a professional man, the kind of service he renders can readily be interpreted in terms of community need. In one doctor's family, the inevitable disrupting of family plans was often to be borne only because people really needed Daddy at the hospital. If this need had not been made a real thing, and if Daddy's help had not been felt to have an importance that somehow dwarfed one's own desire, having to postpone a trip or treat would have been much harder. As it was, one did have the compensation of having helped, too, by not fussing when the plans had to be changed.

If Father holds a business position, some knowledge of the importance of this business to the community is worth having. One needs to know more than that Father "goes to the office" every morning; one certainly needs to know more than that Father "goes to the office to make money." Even the four-year-old can be told in simple terms what Father's job is, and what contribution it makes. If his job is linked directly to the community in which one lives, it is easier to realize its contribution. The personal interest attached to Father's job will do much to make the working together into which it fits more real. Many jobs, to be sure, will not have such obvious and immediate connections. Father often works in another place altogether, and his job is concerned with remote and not easily perceived ends. Even so, we can try to interpret the work we do in terms of the contribution it makes to life as a whole.

Sometimes the committee work of a mother gives an opportunity for allying children with group activity. There may be some small jobs that they can do in order that Red Cross soliciting, the selling of anti-tuberculosis stamps, or the raising of funds for a hospital can go more smoothly. If children are expected to help in the household tasks while Mother is busy in this way, it can be with the idea that this is their share.

Most of us are not active members of a political party except at election time. It is one of our unfortunate peculiarities that politics is so largely left in the hands of professional politicians. However, there are usually civic groups, discussion groups, and the like that have to do with shaping community policy. By taking part, we can give the all-important function of political action a more direct place in our lives. Even though the nine-year-old does not grasp all that goes on in these groups, he can be given some vicarious share in what they are trying to do.

When elections are due, we can give children a sense of their importance and an understanding of how they work. Local issues often touch one nearly enough to have meaning, even to a young child. We must be careful, however, that they are interpreted for him in community terms, not personal ones. The laying of a new sewer may add to Father's taxes, but it may also mean better community housekeeping. By investigating pros and cons ourselves, and by helping children understand them, we can make political activity a real and important part of their concept of social responsibility.

Groups whose purpose is purely recreational also make their contribution to a sense of working together. The Bridge Club whose sole purpose is an afternoon's enjoyment for a few ladies is not much help here, but the Dramatic Club that gives community entertainments is. For children, such groups may provide the salutary experience of seeing Father or Mother in a new setting. One little girl was much impressed with her Father's performance on the stage, and more so by the applause it received.

"My Daddy was the best," she remarked. "I thought only Mummy and I knew that—but the other people thought so, too!"

Community groups to which both children and parents belong. The groups to which all members of a family can belong have the most to contribute for our purposes. The school and the church are such groups. These institutions cut across artificial social barriers as well as across age differences. They represent a diverse community or neighborhood perhaps more effectively than do any other groups.

As soon as children are old enough to go to school, this important social agency becomes a real part of the family. Because it ties up so closely with home, and at the same time makes so many community contacts, the school group offers us unique opportunities. School can be the place where not only children, but parents, go. It can be the channel through which not only parents, but children, make community contributions.

The child who goes to school enters a world that is primarily his. His parents enter it through him. This gives him a new status and a new importance. Here, for the first time, he becomes part of a social group on his own. If we want him to savor this importance properly, however, the part of school to which he belongs must be all his. That is, class-room responsibilities are not a parent's, but a child's. Homework, for instance, is something that concerns a child and his teacher. Help on details of research or explanations of puzzling bits is quite in order,

The child who goes to school enters a world that is primarily his.
His parents enter it through him.

but one ought not to assume any responsibility for getting the job itself done. Any youngster who is old enough to have outside assignments of work is also old enough to learn how to arrange his time so that they get done. Interference here is unfair to him.

There may be occasions when interference between pupil and teacher seems advisable. Parents feel that they know their children so much better than other people do. They may feel that some interpretation of their child is necessary. If such an occasion does arise, the consultation can take place without a child's knowledge. If he gets the idea that what doesn't suit him at school can be fixed up for him by a sympathetic parent, he will not be acting independently in this group.

Most schools, however, have the machinery for the kind of active participation that parents can give. Parent-teacher organizations have the opportunity to do many important community jobs. Their province, the nurture and education of children, is so basic in the life of any community that its scope comes to include most constructive community endeavor. Where they have proved themselves capable, these organizations have been turned to for help by many social agencies. Projects for community health, for recreation, for social welfare, for adult education, call upon the parent-teacher group for assistance. If there is an active organization of this kind in a community, all parents owe it their support; if such an organization is not active, it should be made so. For through the schools, each working in their own sphere, parents and children can genuinely work together for community betterment.

The program of a church often includes opportunities similar to those of the school for useful social functioning. Many of us fail to be consistent in this matter of church membership, for one reason or another. Perhaps it is because the relationship between a church and religion is often confused. Religion, if by that term is meant the way in which philosophical concepts influence behavior and determine values, has been considered a personal matter by many people since the Reformation. Churches are social organizations of fellowship participated in by individuals who think similarly about their religion. Whether one belongs to a church or not may have little to do with one's religion. However, if one does belong, it seems only fair to participate actively in a church's fellowship. For some families, church membership may form a valuable link with the community in which they live. For others, it may not. If it is considered valuable, however, it works best as a family affair. Sending children to a church-school on their own is merely begging the issue. The church-school, it is argued, teaches religion, and religion is something that children should know about. But "teaching religion," by which is usually meant teaching a scale of values, an ethic, is something that we do much more effectively ourselves than it can possibly be done in a church-school, whether we are willing to acknowledge the fact or not. The church-school can supplement. If it is genuinely supplementing the home program, then there is no reason why one should not make the most of this opportunity for participating in a group to which all members of a family can belong.

Community groups to which children themselves belong. There are social groups designed especially for children. The Girl and Boy Scouts are good representatives of these. Troops, of course, differ widely in program and emphasis, but many of them do make a place for community activity that has immediate interest and worth. One local troop of boys became concerned about the careless way in which picnickers were using a stretch of woods that was a favorite haunt of theirs. They devoted an entire Saturday to cleaning it up. Then they posted signs in a few conspicuous places that read as follows: "Other people like to have picnics, too. Please clean up yours. Thank you. The Scouts. Troop——." This appeal got results, and the woods were kept in much better shape, thanks to the concern of the Scouts.

It is worth while to interest one's self in some of these children's groups, find out something about their programs, and give the best of them encouragement. There are many community jobs with which young adolescents can help, if they are given the chance. The sooner youngsters feel that community problems are their concern, and that they can do something about them through their own groups, the better. The community emphasis of a young people's group can do a lot to harness youthful enthusiasm and put it to work in challenging as well as useful ways.

Other ways of participating in community aid. There are a number of ways in which even young children can be given a sense of helping out, of doing something about the evident needs of a community. Sometimes the opportunities come through group affiliations, through appeals made to a church or school. Sometimes one can discover ways of helping independently. Regular responsibility in regard to some immediate community need, no matter how small, is much more worth while from the contributor's point of view than an occasional donation to some more remote cause—though these are necessary, too. Every family can find some need in its surroundings toward which a continuous responsibility can be assumed. Perhaps a few suggestions will be helpful in pointing these out.

The children's ward of a hospital can always find use for toys and picture books. So can a day nursery. Toy appeals are made as Christmas approaches, but one's response to these usually amounts to little more than a collection of discards that Mother takes the initiative in packing up and delivering. Done this way, it gives the six-year-old little sense of actually having made a contribution. He scarcely notices that the truck he never used because its wheels stuck has disappeared from the closet shelf. If, on the other hand, a contact with some place that can use a steady supply of toys is made, the scrapbooks and box-toys that are made as a rainy afternoon's occupation can be contributed regularly. Sometimes one can visit the ward or nursery where these things are used. Making them one's self, for the children one has seen and talked with, gives an added meaning to this sharing of resources, this supplying of needs.

Older children can sometimes help on the sewing that these places always need done. They can raise funds for some special necessity. Two nine-year-old youngsters collected old magazines from their neighborhood, and with the money their sale brought, the piano of a local nursery was tuned and put in shape.

Contact with such local agencies as an anti-tuberculosis association, the Salvation Army, a family welfare organization, a settlement house, may reveal possibilities for help of this kind. If a tangible contribution in the shape of something made or done is possible, so much the better. If money is the only channel through which a contribution can be made, it is well to have it mean something in terms of time and energy on the part of children themselves, as in the collecting of the magazines. In this way, the sense of sharing is more immediate. Wherever contributions are made, the program they are intended to help should be explained. One can not genuinely share unless one can imagine, to some extent at least, the needs this sharing meets.

The importance of a community emphasis. If children feel from the very first that they belong to a community; if they are aware of the historical and cultural heritage, as well as the present functioning, of the place in which they live; if they develop early a sense of functioning within that community themselves—then, from the very first, channels for continuous growing will be open to them. Individual growing extends into the community. Only within a democratic framework is this possible. Communities may contain incongruities and social blind spots, but if they are essentially democratic in structure, the challenge to ever-increasing maturity, to continuous growing, exists.

The person who has been able to ally himself and his interests in some constructive way with the community is sincerely honored by those who know him and are familiar with his work. Such work may have far-reaching effects, or it may be merely a routine job that has to be done; it may be directly concerned with community functioning, or it may be the development of an individual talent. No matter how limited or how seemingly personal it is, however, all our work can be done with a community emphasis, with the threads that lead outward uppermost in mind. Done in this spirit, work has a dignity that reflects upon the worker and is unmistakable to other people, though they may not know its source.

A lot has been said, lately, about power—who shall wield it and what it does to those who do. The person who fulfils himself through his contributions to the community is sharing power. Shared power is a responsibility and a trust. It does not corrupt. Instead, it gives scope for individual growing as the power that is seized can not do. One has only to compare the two to realize this. The "big man," the autocrat, is little: his person may inspire fear, even a fearful veneration, but it does not inspire respect. The person who identifies himself with the community grows visibly in stature; even those who can not understand him tender him a genuine respect. Not long ago this was illustrated afresh for me. One of the service men of a large city hospital was talking about the doctor who had been that hospital's guiding genius before he died.

"We boys didn't see much of the doctor, he was always so busy," he said, "but we thought an awful lot of him. He was the only one of the doctors that we wouldn't have thought of talking to with our hats on." Yet this man was the kind who slipped unobtrusively in and out of committee rooms and seldom raised his quiet voice. It was not pomposity nor an overbearing manner that brought off the hats. It was respect for his intrinsic character, a character that expressed itself in a service so far-reaching that few of us realized its magnitude until it was no longer there.

It is this kind of growing that a community emphasis encourages. All the attitudes we have been exploring previously have their culmination in this community emphasis. Understanding and appreciating the people who surround one are essential to it; using machines as tools, evaluating their use in terms of individual growing, likewise contribute to collective growing; a deep-rooted sense of our human place in nature is a necessary foundation for worthwhile social functioning. Ideally, democratic living is a give-and-take affair. The social structure provides a growing environment for individuals; in return, society demands the best of individual endeavor for the social good. Helping children develop the basic attitudes we have been exploring may do more than anything else to bring us nearer this ideal of democracy.

392.5
A218m

309.1
C687

301.15
A411r

392.5
D983

301.15
A939

392.
B853

392.5
B787m

301.15
A939

392
B884c

392.5
C257b

323.35
S822A

Index

(1)